C000254457

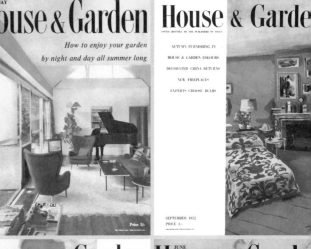

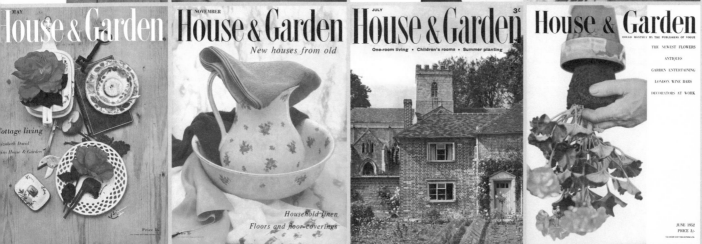

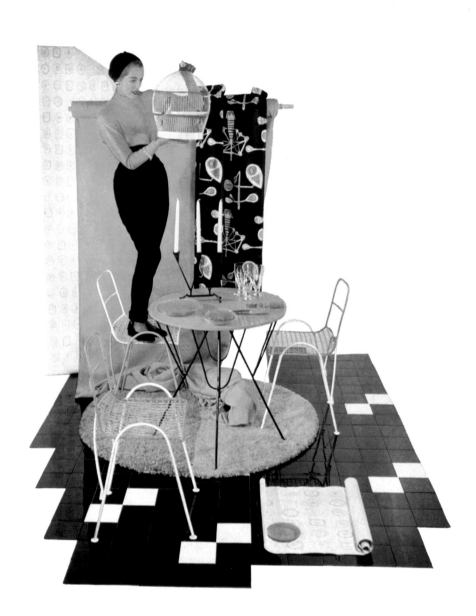

FIFTIES HOUSE

HOUSE & GARDEN

Catriona Gray
Foreword by Terence Conran

conran OCTOPUS

CONTENTS

FOREWORD

BY TERENCE CONRAN

If the Sixties was the time Britain threw off the shackles of grim, post-war austerity then the Fifties was the decade we began picking the lock. It was an important time in the evolution of our nation's tastes but perhaps the influence only became visible a decade later. The seeds of the 'Swinging Sixties' and all its spirit of revolutionary fervour were certainly sown in the 1950s, which is why this book is such an interesting and important record of the British home.

Things were grim in post-war Britain and there were no 'designers' in those days, just a handful of young upstarts rather patronizingly referred to as 'industrial artists'. I personally think that the 'Britain Can Make It' exhibition, at the Victoria & Albert Museum in 1946, was the moment that the UK saw that modernism could lead to a better quality of life, but it takes a long time to get through the sieve of retailers and public, government and royal opinion. Several years later The Festival of Britain gave the country another kick start and enthused people about the possibilities available to them. That is what we tapped into as designers.

There was a younger generation growing up who for the first time had a bit of money in their pockets and wanted to live a life different to that of their parents – and that life most certainly included the way that they decorated their homes. One of the delights of this book, for me, is seeing these two cultures clash and rub against each other, all perfectly recorded by that wonderful magazine, *House & Garden*. As the decade progresses and the story is told you can literally see the nation enjoying and embracing its first glimpses of modernism.

The Fifties was a turning point in the design world and designers were influenced by the innovation seen in the manufacture of new materials. In the UK, at the start of the decade, all you could buy in furniture was shiny reproduction Georgian pieces or huge cocktail cabinets that looked like glossy, veneered, bucolic charladies, but a remarkable collection of architects and designers on the West Coast of the US was emerging, including George Nelson, Eero Saarinen, Alexander Girard, and particularly Charles and Ray Eames. They produced amazing home furnishings egged on by the wonderful *Arts & Architecture* magazine, which was our bible at that time. The increasing influence of these designers and architects is an important part of this book.

And of course that design bible of our own, *House & Garden*, was recording these changes. I will always be indebted to the magazine as it gave me my first ever piece of publicity when I was just nineteen. I had a very small room in a house in Warwick Gardens next to Olive Sullivan who was then decorating editor of *House & Garden*. Her room was very pretty, filled with rosebuds and femininity, whereas mine was about as different as could be! It was filled with my own welded metal furniture, bright colours and Paolozzi prints and pretty uncomfortable. But *House & Garden* featured it and it helped me start my own career in home furnishings.

Right
Terence Conran in 1956, sitting in a 'Dog Basket' chair of his own design.

Following pages, clockwise from top left
A 1950 bride surveys her practical dining room, with oak furniture from Dunns, rush matting and an occasional table from Heal's (foreground). John Piper works on his huge mural for the outside of the Homes and Gardens pavilion on the Festival of Britain site. A 1959 feature urged for the return of the 'what-not' with 18th- and 19th-century antiques and contemporary glass from Finmar and Liberty. Louis le Brocquy's studio in 1953, with Ercol furniture alongside his easels, books and painting equipment; on the wall is *A Family* (1951), from his 'Grey' period.

INTRODUCTION

'A good deal of philosophical thought has been given to the problem of here and now. Without ranging into the metaphysics of Dunne's serial universe, one can still remain fascinated by the particular passing moment that is here and then gone for ever, leaving its imprint only on film and wax and steel tape and the printed page. In a magazine like House & Garden, *in an issue such as this, there lies, hidden to us who are so close to today, the evidence that will speak to another generation of our way of life, of the sort of people that we were in the 1950s.'*

— JULY 1957

These words were written as an introduction to a feature on a modern house – designed by *House & Garden* – that epitomized all that was current and fashionable in the mid-Fifties. The six decades that have elapsed since then have dulled the memory of the Fifties interior, but have also imbued magazines such as *House & Garden* with an invaluable importance, as they narrate a social and aesthetic history that would otherwise be lost. As an internationally renowned design magazine, *House & Garden* created and chronicled trends, and within its pages lies a complete record of what well-designed homes really looked like. Its fascination with the passing moment succeeded in preserving it, and this diverse set of photographs taken from the magazine's archive offers an immediate, intimate view of the world's most stylish interiors during this decade of innovation and experimentation.

The Fifties saw a radical change in interior design. This was due to several reasons: the rising popularity of modernist architecture and furniture; the increased availability of new materials and technology; and the social change created by the huge upheaval occasioned by two world wars. Modernism was nothing new in the Fifties; in terms of design, it was the pioneering work of the Bauhaus movement in the Thirties that had popularized this style. However, since trends in interiors move at a slightly slower pace than fashion – you change your clothes more frequently than you do your furniture, after all – this stripped-back, sparse aesthetic hadn't fully caught on. In Britain, much of this was due to the Second World War. With rationing in place, houses under the threat of bombing and all available resources being channelled into the war effort, interior decoration was put on ice in the years during and immediately after the war. A 'make do and mend' mentality abounded, and any furniture bought new between 1943 and 1952 was likely to be government-sanctioned Utility furniture. This furniture came in a very limited range of designs, and its sparse functionality was clearly influenced by the Bauhaus style. However, it was not particularly popular with the public, so, when design restrictions were finally lifted in 1952, there was an explosion of interest in fresh, new styles of furniture design.

The start of the Fifties also saw a desperate need for new housing. Approximately one-third of British houses had been seriously damaged or demolished during the war, which meant that housing was an urgent priority. The housing shortage was exacerbated by an increase in marriages and births – the Fifties saw a baby boom – so house building was a national concern throughout the decade. This regeneration process in the wake of the Second World War saw the principles of modern architects being given free rein, and a new style of architecture emerged, creating the Britain that we recognize today.

A need for economy meant that these new homes were smaller than their predecessors and contained fewer rooms. This completely transformed how houses were laid out. Traditionally, houses had been built with numerous rooms, each with a very specific purpose and which might have been used only at certain times of the day. Architects began to question the need for multiple

spaces for sitting or dining, favouring larger rooms that could be used as more general living areas. It was during this decade that open-plan interiors first became popular.

More than any other event, the 1951 Festival of Britain kick-started a new era of design. It was planned as a morale-boosting project to aid recovery after the war and to show the British public what the future held – it was a celebration of culture and British history, industry, hopes and identity. Lauded as a 'tonic to the nation' by its director, Gerald Barry, the festival stimulated British manufacturing industries and sparked an interest in technological developments that were relevant to everyone. Eight and a half million people visited the festival, located in the newly built Royal Festival Hall on London's South Bank, between May and September 1951. Its cultural influence spread throughout the country, as other cities and towns were encouraged to organize events and exhibitions to celebrate the festival.

The festival showcased the world of well-known designers in the fields of textile, furniture and industrial design, and it also suggested ways in which people could update and modernize their own homes. It sparked a desire for new, innovative design, and was well timed to coincide with the economic growth that gave people a purchasing power not seen since before the outbreak of war; televisions, washing machines and refrigerators were becoming standard items for every home. Modernism suffused the air and found its way into the country's interiors.

Throughout this decade British *House & Garden* not only recorded, but pioneered,

Above
A *House & Garden* cover from March 1951 introducing the new *House & Garden* colour range, which became a popular commercial enterprise throughout the Fifties.

this rapidly changing design aesthetic. Notable contributors included Nancy Mitford, Vita Sackville-West and John Betjeman, while Elizabeth David had a regular food column. Each month, the decoration pages compiled montages of homewares and furniture from exciting new designers such as Charles and Ray Eames, Jean Prouvé and George Nakashima.

Collaborations with advertisers boomed during the Fifties, and substantial advertorials were run in the front of each issue in full colour, showcasing furniture from Heal's and other leading design companies. Often, a number of different advertisers were used in these room schemes, so they have an eclectic, more realistic quality that is not found in standard advertising shots. These room schemes were all built in the *Vogue* studios and shot by Condé Nast's in-house photographers.

In 1956 and 1957 *House & Garden* planned its ideal modern house, from its design to its decoration. The 'House of Ideas' – both the 1956 and the 1957 versions – is a unique photographic record of what the ideal Fifties house should look like, both internally and externally. The photographs and the accompanying text describe the project from start to finish and offer a fantastic insight into the process of creating a house that was entirely of its time. Part One of this book explores the different rooms of the Fifties house and considers how these spaces were used in contrast to their predecessors. Part Two looks at the more practical application of these trends. Twelve houses that were featured in the magazine are discussed as case studies, showing the innovative vision of the owners, many of who were notable designers and architects. The final part of the book focuses upon interior details, showing the popular styles of furniture, textiles, flooring and wallcoverings that helped to characterize the Fifties interior. The extraordinary breadth of this material shows, with complete authenticity, how trends emerged and developed over the course of this extraordinary decade.

'EASY WAYS TO EASIER LIVING'

APRIL 1954

'Don't grope in the dark; paint the light switches with luminous paint, especially in dark corridors and the bathroom. Such paint is also good for fuse boxes, gas taps, the inside of the cellar door, etc.

Make a ferociously efficient shoe-scraper from metal bottle caps nailed upside down on a board, in your own initials or a pretty pattern.

Find chemistry flasks for oil and vinegar, and a huge one for wine.

Stuff a giant brandy glass with carnation heads.

Be bold with napkins; have each a different colour.

Many washing machines make good dirty-clothes bins.

Why not have a switch near the floor so that you can turn off the light with your foot when you're carrying a tray?

A large kitchen table, covered in black and white diamond linoleum, makes a decorative family meal table.

A goldfish tank is a good decoration in the bathroom.

Pad your lavatory seat with bright-coloured towelling.

What colour will your walls be when the matt paint or distemper dries out? Try it first on clean white blotting paper: almost at once the shine goes and you can see exactly what it will look like.

Strain lumps and impurities from paint and wallpaper paste through old laddered nylons.

Back shelves with mirror to double your decorative displays.

Line all your cosmetic drawers with amenable, unabusable plastic.'

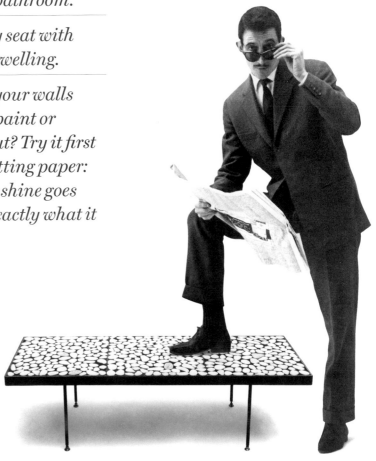

Right
A racy-looking gentleman eyes up the reader in this 1959 shopping shoot. However, the shoot's real star is the Heal's coffee table, with a metal frame and a black-and-white pebble top.

1. ROOMS

62

THE
FIFTIES
BEDSIT & STUDIO
BEDROOM

76

THE
FIFTIES
BEDROOM

90

THE
FIFTIES
BATHROOM

THE FIFTIES KITCHEN

'Here they are, pages and pages of the very newest in trans-Atlantic kitchens, each a glowing picture singing of the joys of Home, Home on the Range.'

—MARCH 1958

Left
Compact, built-in storage makes the most of the limited space in this 1953 kitchen. The Prescold refrigerator incorporates a freezer unit, while the black and white floor tiles complement the fitted units and provide a neutral foil for the bright walls. The wall lights, chosen to balance this careful colour scheme, were made by Troughton & Young and could be adjusted to provide uplighting or downlighting, as required.

Right
Although the grey tiles and white, plastic-coated units create a cool base tone in this 1952 kitchen, cherry-coloured kitchen utensils add vibrant colour, as do the matching stools from Lennon. Pattern also plays a part, found in the strip of Sanderson wallpaper that enlivens the wall above the tiles and in the curtain fabric that was designed by Roger Nicholson for Whitehead. Another focal point is the ironing board – a new design by Beldray, made out of perforated steel to keep it cool.

Left

The bold red of these wooden units adds drama to this 1953 kitchen, and flush handles emphasize the modern look. A pull-out wooden chopping board slides underneath an enamel work surface, while an extractor fan over the range removes cooking smells and incorporates a shelf used for warming plates. The bright-red casserole dish on the gas hob

was typical of the growing trend for cooking vessels that could double as tableware. The original kitchen plan showed how the kitchen had been carefully designed to make the most of space – the laundry appliances are grouped together at one end of the room, while the range at the other end is conveniently close to the serving hatch.

Below

This page is taken from a February 1951 article entitled 'What's Old in Electric Cookers?' which compared the newest innovations in electric cookers with their Thirties counterparts. In the early Fifties, cookers came in different sizes to suit a variety of households. The model at the top, designed for a family of two, shows how Creda updated its smallest cooker to

reflect modern design. Below, a heavy cast-iron Carron cooker from the Thirties was updated to include a glass door and a separate rack for a plug-in kettle.

The modern fitted kitchen had first appeared in the States, and during the Fifties American-style fitted kitchens acquired an international following. Kitchens transformed from being a functional – if somewhat uninspiring – room, to the heart of the house. By the Fifties, live-in help was virtually unheard of in all but the wealthiest homes. Instead, it was expected that the homeowner would do the bulk of the housework and cooking. Although this had long been the situation in working-class households, this was a new development for the professional classes. An economical 'do it yourself' spirit prevailed in this decade, a relic of the Second World War, and this became manifest in men taking an interest in home improvements and in an expectation that women would be hands-on homemakers. Because the homeowners were spending far more time in the kitchen than in previous generations, it made sense that, for the first time, this room became a hub for design trends.

For a family of two

Below: The early version of Creda's little cooker had awkward cabriole legs, and jutting corners, and it was altogether an ungainly design. Its colouring was dark, and its shape difficult to fit in with other equipment. The solid plate was slower to heat up than is the new radiant one

Left: Eighteen inches square, the Creda Cadet has a small oven with a grill, and a plate-warming cupboard. As on the other cookers, this oven is regulated by thermostat; the boiling plate has variable heat control. The cooker can be plugged into any power point. £15 10s. Stand, 25s. 6d.

For a family of four

Below: The Carron cooker, in the 'thirties, had many protruding and dirt-catching angles, hinges and handles. Beneath it there was only unusable floor space which was difficult to sweep (now the space can be filled by a heated drawer for plates); and there was no room suitable for a kettle

Right: Today's Carron has an outlet for your kettle, and a rack to place it on; a glass door so that you can see into oven; lights on the splash-back that show which boiling plates are on; well-sprung doors. Its standard size fits in with any kitchen units. £34 8s. 6d. including extras shown

Below

Terence Conran designed this informal 1953 kitchen, which features a minimal island unit that cleverly combines a table and a shelf. The table has the advantage of doubling as an extra surface for preparing food. The stools are from Liberty. This kitchen also has state-of-the-art built-in units, which are topped with steel-blue Formica. Although the

flush handles of the fitted units are typical of the time, the gas cooker still has the unwieldly knobs that were quickly becoming very outdated.

Right

Both the cooker and the refrigerator in this 1953 kitchen are from GEC, a Birmingham-based company that had made many of the early models of electric cookers. Despite the modern Troughton & Young lights, the overall impression of this kitchen is rather dull, the main culprit being the mottled linoleum floor tiles. The coated fabric that covers the

end wall and the top of the stool also has a somewhat deadening effect, although matters aren't helped by the rather up-front style of food photography that was popular at the time.

In urban, middle-class houses, the kitchen was transformed into a public rather than a private space. New architectural plans began to incorporate the dining room into the kitchen, so for the first time it was a place to entertain guests as well as a food-preparation area. This was partly a practical solution – if the hostess was in the kitchen, it made things difficult if the dining area was in a different part of the house.

Cooking was rendered easier by improved technology. Although the Aga had been around since the Thirties, it became fashionable and more easily obtainable and could also heat water as well as cook food. Electric cookers became more sophisticated than their Thirties counterparts; they were also relatively cheap by comparison, which meant that more households could afford them. It was far from ideal however – cooker thermostats still weren't properly regulated at the start of the decade, which meant that cooking times could vary wildly depending on the individual cooker.

Left

This 1954 kitchen is an example of clever space planning, as it was required to double as a laundry, despite being of quite compact dimensions. The most interesting piece is the very modern drying rack. Custom-made by M & C Wickham furniture, its design echoes that of Charles and Ray Eames's iconic 'Hang It All' coat rack that had been released the previous year. Plain black linoleum flooring and black and blue Formica work surfaces, alongside the white kitchen units and metal venetian blinds, transform a domestic space into something resolutely modern. The chair is by Ernest Race while the 'Lennon' stool is from Heal's.

Above

Don't let yourself get distracted by the red-and-white striped 'Ventilator Awning' by The Artistic Blind Co. It may be an utterly unexpected take on the traditional extractor fan, but to the right of this 1955 picture is something equally unusual: a Fifties dishwasher. Amazingly, this Adamaid automatic dishwasher was able to wash, rinse and dry utensils in three minutes. With such innovative examples of Fifties technology, it's all too easy to overlook the cleverly cut linoleum floor that links the entire scheme together.

The balance between the deep-plum walls and the white of the woodwork, electrical goods and lights lends this 1955 kitchen a sophisticated style. While the pine units are not fashionable by today's standard, the flush handles and the pale wood made a dramatic and refreshing change from the heavy dark wood of the preceding decade. This American-style kitchen manages to create an urbane atmosphere and could easily double as a space for entertaining.

This compact 1955 kitchen was part of a fashionable lady's Knightsbridge flat. Because of the small space, and because it was more frequently used to prepare a simple snack as opposed to heavy catering, it is fitted out with a two-ring gas hob to save space. The owner's primary concern was that the kitchen should look stylish when the dining-room door was ajar, so the surfaces are topped in red Wareite and the handles of the fitted units and the patterned wallpaper were chosen to match.

Below
The architect owner cleverly designed this 1955 kitchen to squeeze into a corridor. Because of the lack of windows, ventilation was vital, hence the large extractor fan built into the ceiling. Storage racks above the cooker neatly house pots and pans, while white kitchen units blend into the wall behind them. Cream and red tiles are continued in the

bathroom beyond, which visually extends the space and prevents it from feeling too confined.

Kitchen units were being mass-produced and lauded for their space- and time-saving design. They enabled all the kitchen appliances to be fitted neatly into a compact area and had the added benefit of incorporating storage space. The fitted kitchen felt modern because of its coherent design; cupboards made full use of wall space above and below the work surface, while the flush finishes were easier to clean – they stopped dust and dirt falling down the side of fitted appliances. Stainless-steel sinks became popular. They could be fitted into the new kitchen units and gradually replaced their heavy ceramic predecessors. Refrigerators became much more widely used and were available in a variety of colours; the term 'white goods' had yet to be coined in the Fifties. In council (public) housing, refrigerators were fitted as standard and rented out to tenants, while in private homes they also became

Above
The wallpaper in this 1955 kitchen in Belgravia was typical of the decade. It has a culinary motif, incorporating forks and lobsters. The cream Nevastane units have dramatic red handles, and the surfaces are topped with a durable red plastic, with a black edging. A line of open storage compartments enabled the cook to easily access kitchen essentials such as condiments and spices.

Right
This 1955 kitchen incorporates many of the hallmarks of Fifties design. It uses lots of black and white, most notably in the black-and-white chequered linoleum floor tiles. One wall is painted bright red, while other accents of colour are created by the blue-painted chair from Buoyant and the mustard carpet in the dining area. A boiler by Crane Carlton, compatible with solid-fuel or oil, was used to provide central heating.

Right
The kitchen units in this 1955 room scheme
are from Nevastane (as on page 24). The
bright walls are in 'Lemon Peel', a colour
chosen from the *House & Garden* 1955
colour collection. The dining area
incorporates a golden-yellow carpet chosen
to complement the walls and blond-wood
furniture. A 'Bubble' design two-tone
pendant shade is from Rotaflex Lighting,
its modern design slightly eclipsed by the
Harper's '1500 Food Mincer', included
because of its rubber feet, which eliminated
the need for clamping the mincer to
the table.

very popular, although in rural areas many
households still relied on the larder to keep
food cool.

As almost all homes had electricity, a new
wave of kitchen appliances flooded on to the
market. Electric kettles, electric mixers and
toasters with in-built timers were all lauded
as devices to make food preparation easier
and more efficient. Bright colours were in
fashion and kitchen design embraced this
vibrant mood. Flooring was cheap and
cheerful; the most popular choices were
cork tiles or linoleum – often patterned
rather than plain in order to camouflage
dirt. Primary colours were popular and new
materials were used, as these could be kept
clean and were easy to maintain. Plastics
and PVC, linoleum and laminates could be
easily produced in a wide range of colours,
and it was considered perfectly acceptable
to have several bright colours clashing in a
single interior; yellows, reds and oranges
were all very popular during this decade.
There was also a desire to substitute
traditional materials with more innovative
ones. Some of these developments, such
as Formica worktops, are still popular
today. Other innovations, such as PVC
curtains, have not aged quite so well.
Formica was incredibly popular throughout
this decade, as it was durable and heat
resistant. It came in a variety of colours and
patterns, and looked cheerful and modern.
Kitchen fabrics came in bold patterns and
often had food-related motifs. Glasses
of wine, vegetables such as aubergines,

Below
Similar to today's kitchens, this 1957 room doubles as a space to do laundry as well as cook. A small cerulean-and-white Servis washing machine is next to the refrigerator, which is built into a floor-to-ceiling storage unit. To the left is an airing cupboard, while the gas cooker is the Parkinson 'Renown Six'. The lemon yellow and white stools are from Conran.

'Cinderella would have stayed at home if her fairy godmother had first conjured up all this kitchen equipment' was the headline of this 1957 piece on colourful kitchen utensils. The three multi-toned saucepans are Jury Jetware, and the Hillamix liquidizer incorporates a coffee grinder. The brown-and-blue bowl is a 'Tipmix' bowl from Wearside Pottery, which stood firmly if tilted; the golden casserole is from Worcester; while the set of blue 'Bex' measuring cups are by Halex. At the centre are the 'Waymaster' kitchen scales by Precision Engineering, which were manufactured in seven different colours.

and ingredients such as pasta were then seen as exotic items and were celebrated in collections of kitchen textiles and wallpapers. Wallpapers designed especially for kitchens were frequently adorned with slices of fruit, vegetables or fish – a trend that originally started in the States but soon spread to Britain.

A particularly popular place to show off your Formica was on an island unit – another Fifties trend – which was often used to make a division between the kitchen and dining area. Many of these island units had rounded ends to give them a more futuristic look and were convenient as an additional area for preparing food. They were also used to display tableware – studio-type pottery was in fashion, and was either handmade or else machine-produced to look handmade. Much of it was inspired by Scandinavian styles, with gourd shapes and glazes that looked hand-finished. British manufacturers were quick to adopt this trend and made similar items. This gradual coming-together of cooking and dining areas resulted in new, attractive ranges of pots and dishes that could be brought straight from oven to table, and also had the virtue of cutting down on the washing-up. Despite the vogue for newfangled kitchen appliances, it would take several more decades for dishwashers to become a standard household item.

Left

This 'newlywed's dream kitchen' was thought out in 1959 by Elizabeth Campbell, pictured here, who was a recently married member of *House & Garden*'s editorial staff. It includes a Tricity hob, eye-level oven and a Prescold refrigerator, and is brightly decorated with work surfaces in two different colours of Formica . The washable wallpaper is from Crown. Although the white coffee cups and glass tumblers on the table may be from Finnish Design, the 'Blue Italian' Spode earthenware was made a little closer to home.

Right

This 'Easylux' grocery cabinet was imported by Dahl Bros and was stocked by Liberty. By 1959, the use of clear plastic had become popular in kitchen utensils and storage as a hard-wearing and easy-to-clean material. The use of it in this cabinet enabled the cook to easily see what was stored in each compartment. Mounted against its punched-metal background, it plays upon the fashion for using science-inspired designs in a domestic setting.

THE FIFTIES SITTING ROOM

'Back your own taste and judgement. Have no fear. In making experiments, you will make mistakes, but gradually, your own two eyes will tell you what is wrong. That way come judgement and assurance. There is no other way. Nobody, I am sure, was born with quite impeccable taste. So go to it!'

—SEPTEMBER 1958

Left
This 1952 sitting room was designed to have a country feel not traditionally associated with the interior decoration of a modern house. You can tell it is modern because of the horizontal shape of the window and the simple softwood window sill. The furniture is all from Ercol's 'Windsor' collection and has been upholstered in a striped fabric. The Sanderson 'Trellis' wallpaper is in cinnamon and white on a blue ground. Mohair rugs from Field's are in two *House & Garden* colours from the 1952 collection – 'Cherry' and 'Avocado'. The lamps are from H C Hiscock.

Right
Aside from wondering why the model in the picture is sitting on the floor when there are so many vacant chairs to choose from, the most striking thing about this 1954 shot is the yellow-and-brown chair covers. These use a Sanderson fabric, 'Blitz', a screen-printed cotton in an abstract design. A note in the accompanying caption reads 'Patterns of covers gladly sent on request'. The furniture, along with the china, is all from Harrison Gibson. Much is made of the metal venetian blinds, then seen as being super stylish and the height of modernity.

Below left
The small dimensions of the 'Ace' television set enabled it to be concealed within a walnut cabinet in this 1953 sitting room. The geometric wallpaper and cotton-mix upholstery fabrics are both by Sanderson and match the strong colour of the 'Forest Green' paint on the wall behind the television.

Below right
Bright linoleum flooring makes a statement in this 1953 dining and sitting room, which features an unusual piece of wall art fashioned out of kitchen utensils. The shelving unit is by Terence Conran, and the slim metal vertical supports complement the black metal legs of the custom-built stools and table.

Right
Enthusiasts of Mid-century design will doubtlessly recognize the two chairs that add a resolutely modern note to this 1952 sitting room. They were designed by Robin Day, for furniture company Hille & Co. Hille still manufactures furniture designed by Day, although this particular model is not currently in production. The settee is another Robin Day design, while the rest of the furniture comes from the 'Unad' collection by Story. The wallpaper and fabric are by Sanderson – throughout the Fifties, the company was a major advertiser in *House & Garden*, so its products featured heavily in these studio shots.

With the influx of modern furniture, bright colours and boldly patterned textiles, the sitting room became the first room to reflect the emerging design trends that were eagerly adopted by a public sick of wartime shortages. There was a construction boom in the years after the Second World War; new houses tended to be smaller, with fewer rooms, so the sitting room replaced the drawing room as the primary space for entertaining visitors as well as for family living. Even in older houses, the desire for a more open-plan layout resulted in a growing tendency towards a larger, multipurpose living space that was used to relax, entertain, play, eat and work.

Advances in heating meant that the traditional layout of the sitting room altered. Before, chairs were grouped around the fire, which was the primary focus of the room. Although older houses still used solid-fuel fires in the sitting room, central heating was gradually becoming more prevalent and was being installed as standard in new builds. Wood-burning stoves became a widespread alternative to open fires as they were cleaner and more efficient. Underfloor heating was also popular, while a less successful innovation was ceiling heating. It was supposed to mimic the warming effects of sunlight, but in practice people's heads became overheated, so it was never widely adopted.

The biggest revolution in the Fifties sitting room was the introduction of the television. At the start of the decade it was

Far left
In this 1953 sitting room, the muted colour of the gunmetal 'Langdon' wallpaper by John Line Wallpaper is lifted by the use of the same paper in a contrasting mustard colourway. Although the curtains are in mustard and red, the overall effect is not overly bright, mainly due to the sobering shade of the olive Wilton carpet. The coffee table is from Liberty, while the metal table lamp is by Troughton & Young. The rest of the furniture is by Horace Holme, and the chair in the foreground is unusually upholstered, with the seat pad in a contrasting shade.

Left
Strong colours characterize this 1952 sitting room. A blue wall sets off the painting, *Light and Shadow*, by Welsh painter Ceri Richards. It also emphasizes the 'Ariel' printed curtains from Edinburgh Weavers. Unusually, a small wooden trellis has been affixed above the mantelpiece to encourage the potted plant to climb it. House plants add life to this sitting room, which opens out to a conservatory. The fireplace surround makes a modern statement using tiles by Peggy Angus. Once again, the ceiling lights are from Troughton & Young – in the 'Versalite' design – while the 'Long John' table is from Liberty.

Below
Modern readers will find little of the rustic about this 1953 room set, which has been styled as a 'country living room'. Instead, Ercol furniture creates a sense of unity throughout the room. The settee and chair are both the 'Bergère' design. The curtains are in 'Miscellany' by Lucienne Day for Celanese-Sanderson, and their pattern complements the fire surround by Pilkington, which manufactured the hand-printed grey tiles with their off-white diaper pattern. An electric heater, then the height of modernity, made in brown plastic (intended to resemble walnut), can be seen on the back wall, next to the rather bulky radio unit.

Right
The 'Tripolina' chairs, covered in cherry and nasturtium canvas, along with the metal-framed dining chairs, linoleum-topped dining table and metal and wood bookcase, are all by Conran Furniture. The 'Harlequin' coffee table, made out of walnut and sycamore, was designed by Herbert Berry. The grey-and-white patterned wallpaper was designed by Lucienne Day for Crown; she also created the pattern for the glazed-cotton fabric to the left of the picture. An unusual splash of colour comes in the form of the lilac-painted ceiling, and a statement wall in cherry red. By contrast, the floor is neutrally attired in white carpet.

still something of a novelty, but by the end of it, the television had become a standard and accessible form of entertainment. From a design perspective, the introduction of the television into the sitting room meant that seating now tended to be grouped around the television set instead of the fire.

Three-piece suites were popular, especially in wingback styles. Robin Day's designs for Hille helped to popularize a new generation of furniture. The heavily upholstered, boxy shapes so common in the Forties were replaced with a trend for slender wooden or metal legs and a more svelte construction. For those brave enough to embrace it, cutting-edge furniture was produced by forward-thinking companies such as Knoll, which brought the work of designers such as Harry Bertoia and Arne Jacobsen to an international audience. The unusual shapes that characterized this new coterie of furniture were emphasized by the brightly coloured upholstery fabrics, which certainly must have made quite an impact after the enforced plainness of the war years in Britain. Although this contrast was less noticeable in the States, the Fifties nonetheless saw a dramatic change in the style of furniture and range of colour palettes used in interior design.

This revolution in furniture design had its effect on the rest of the room. Walls were painted from floor to ceiling in bold colours; patterned wallpaper was popular,

Left
This 1955 design epitomizes an on-trend Fifties sitting room. It is a multi-toned scheme with a contrasting colour, anchored with black and lots of white. The base of the room is two shades of red, one orange-based 'Guardsman' red, the other a dark red with a blue base. 'Clover Pink' and 'Cerulean' striped cushions add contrast, as does the 'Cerulean' seat cover of the antique ebonized chair.

Right
The totem column that forms the focal point of this 1952 sitting room is made from an asbestos flue pipe painted in red, blue and yellow in a geometrical, Mondrian-like design. Nearly all the furniture in this sitting room is second-hand or customized to create an economical, but very modern, space.

Far right
This exotic sitting room was designed by *House & Garden* photographer Anthony Denney, who was decoration editor of *Vogue* when this was shot in 1959. White walls allow his collection of curiosities to be shown off to the full. This sitting room is ahead of its time: as air travel became more popular in the Sixties, interiors increasingly displayed their owners' collections of curios from other cultures and exotic locations.

too, featuring abstract or geometric designs. Fitted carpets were a common choice of floor covering, again often in an eye-catching pattern or bright colour. They were now being made in synthetic fabrics, which made them more accessible, though still costly to purchase, and vacuum cleaners meant that they were easy to clean. Natural materials such as cork tiles or wooden floorboards or parquet were also popular, particularly with aficionados of modern furniture.

Other, subtle changes in interior design included the upsurge in flush door handles that complemented the lines of the modern furniture. These replaced the traditional door knob in new houses and were seen as being more practical, as they could be opened with an elbow – useful for the cook if the sitting room was doubling as a dining area. The way in which the sitting room was lit also changed, in line with the need to use the room as a multipurpose space. Previously, a single, central light with a large lampshade might have been the only source of light, but the increasing number of wall sockets enabled lighting to be more flexible. Central room lights remained but tended to be set at different levels, and the introduction of dimmer switches meant that the strength of light could be varied as required. Uplighting became popular; it had the advantage of eliminating harsh shadows, which led to a softer, more flattering effect. Areas for reading or working were given extra illumination with standard lamps – both traditional and modern designs were used. Antique styles were still popular, although lampshades in frilly fabric were abandoned in favour of plainer, modern styles. Simple shades were made out of cellulose, paper or cloth, while more elaborate, Scandinavian-style versions were fashioned from coloured, hand-blown glass. Metal standard lamps were common,

Below
This small 1955 sitting room is enlivened by the sky-blue walls and draped net curtain in lemon yellow. The furniture makes an equal impact; made by Buoyant, the 'Flair' sofa was composed of three separate sections, upholstered in off-white and a dark navy. This enabled flexible seating that was well suited to a room where space was limited. The brass

and black-wood table lamp, with a pleated silk shade, was made by Hiscock Appleby, as was the matching, twin-shade wall bracket.

Right
This is another example of a room that relied upon a background palette of black and white that acted as a base for pastel tones. In this 1956 example, the walls are painted a sky blue, while the emerald-green seat pads add a richer dose of colour to bring out the warm tones of the wood and cane Danish furniture, preventing the white floor and woodwork

from becoming too pallid. The two oak divider units are by British company E Gomme, which became well known in the Fifties for its G Plan furniture.

and their bold designs were a relatively affordable way of updating a sitting room.

Fabrics could also enliven an interior and were an easy way to add a modern touch with a limited budget. A number of different styles were available. Abstract designs abounded, often with patterns inspired by science – the structure of DNA had been discovered in 1953 and was the inspiration for a number of textile designs. By contrast, pretty sprigged florals were in demand too – today Cath Kidston's signature floral patterns are inspired by Fifties prints. These floral motifs might be set against polka dots or stripes in pinks, reds, blues and yellows. Animal prints were also widespread. Leopard print – popularized by interior designer Madeleine Castaing – and zebra print were considered to be chic, and fur found its way on to rugs, cushions and throws, although, even in the Fifties, fake fur was often used as a substitute for real animal skins.

While the combination of a new era in furniture design and an influx of bright colours changed the look of the sitting room, the most profound changes came from technological advances – most notably in heating and in the introduction of the television – and in the shift towards the sitting room being the single shared living space of the house. All of these changes have become universally accepted today but they all have their origins in the Fifties.

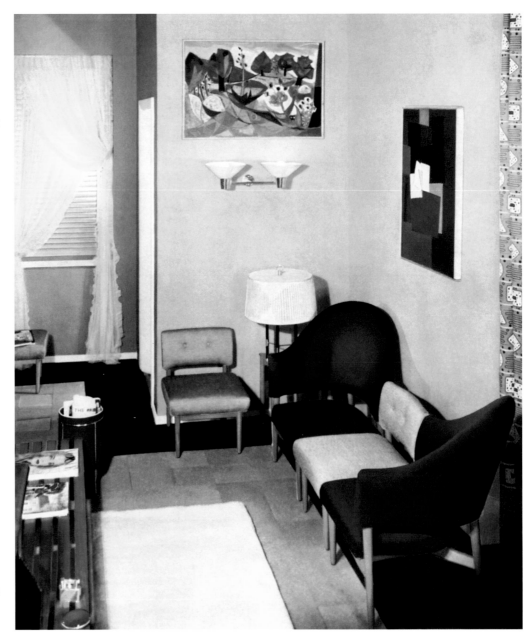

Far left
This 1958 room was used to illustrate an article entitled 'Is Sludge Enough?', which derided the Forties fashion for dull colours and instead advocated bright, vibrant interiors. Although the red curtains and teal upholstery in this sitting room certainly liven things up colour-wise, the real drama is provided by the radical shapes of the two chairs, which were both designed by Harry Bertoia for Knoll. The low wooden table is also from Knoll and was designed by Florence Knoll, who ran the company along with her husband, Hans. An enlarged black-and-white print of a 16th-century portrait hangs on the wall.

Left
In this 1958 room, designed by photographer and *Vogue* decoration editor Anthony Denney, an Axminster carpet in a Turkish design is placed alongside Scandinavian-style furniture and glass, its bold pattern contrasting with the bare white walls. Arne Jacobsen designed the upholstered chair, while the table is composed of six, shield-shaped tables in painted beech that are from Heal's. The Italian glass bottles and coloured-glass tumblers are from Finmar, which was then one of the major importers of Scandinavian furniture and glassware to the UK.

Lilac walls, clashing hues of green upholstery and a chess set left in the middle of a carpet which is designed to imitate the look of rush matting: this 1954 room shows the more eccentric elements of Fifties fashion. Amid this riot of colour, the simple, white tiled fireplace from Pilkington provides a restful focal point, while the clean lines of Robin Day's furniture for Hille work well with the modern art and stop this busy room scheme from looking too fussy. House plants emphasize this room's connection with the tiled outdoor terrace beyond the French windows.

Left
The metal floor-to-ceiling shelving unit provides a modern storage solution in this 1958 house. The shelving is custom-built to place the television set at the centre, while allowing for plenty of space to store books. It also fulfils the role of a side table, with a small collection of spirits sitting beside a bowl of popcorn and above an ashtray, clearly accoutrements for an evening spent in front of the television. Although the 'box' is the firm focal point, interest is added by the bold orange walls and cupboard doors, while the warm tones are continued by the cork floor tiles.

Right
House & Garden photographer, Michael Wickham, designed this family sitting room in 1958. The inherited, mahogany grandfather clock is integrated with modern Scandinavian-style furniture. The teak dining table and chair were designed by Møller of Denmark, while the purple tub chair and the teak and brass Danish chair are both from Heal's. Beside the Woollands sofa is a wire and metal chair designed by Charles Eames, showing that cutting-edge furniture could sit easily alongside family heirlooms.

THE FIFTIES
DINING ROOM

'The grand-opera approach has gone out of entertaining now. Large staffs, lavish larders, and leisure no longer exist for most people. Meals must be prepared with little help, at the last minute, after active days.'

— MAY 1953

Left
This 1957 dining room uses shades from the *House & Garden* colour collection, including the 'Kingfisher Blue' linoleum flooring and the 'Mustard' and 'Sky Blue' panels of wallpaper. The extending table, made from black Australian bean wood, and the china cabinet, are both by Ian Henderson. The bird-print patterned wallpaper is from Wall Paper Manufacturers, and a metal birdcage is placed cleverly in front of it. The dining chairs are 'No.6251', by Vanson.

Right
These furnishings were intended for a modern dining room (c. 1952) and reflect the Fifties taste for blond-wood furniture and patterned fabrics. The result is a lighter, less formal approach to dining. Here, the teak furniture is from the 'Cumbrae' collection by Morris, a British furniture company that is still in existence today. The paint and the wallpaper – the latter in the colourful, freehand, small-scale motifs that were so popular during this decade – are by Cole & Son. The furnishing fabrics are by Old Glamis, a Dundee-based company that exported to an international market throughout the Fifties.

Following pages
This 1957 dining room is resolutely modern. The table and sideboard, with their slim, black metal legs, are from Conran. The fibreglass chairs, in blue, yellow and orange, are by British company Kandya, which had shown its modern designs at the Festival of Britain and whose furniture is now popular with Mid-century collectors. A rice-paper screen is decorated with a butterfly pattern, while on the wall hang two Henry Moore reproductions, *Three Reclining Figures* and Sketches for *Three Standing Figures*, alongside an early Howard Hodgkin. The black-and-white china is from Denby's 'Eclipse' collection.

Left
This photograph is taken from a 1958 series entitled 'Rooms for Your Money', which discussed how best to furnish a room that would last for many years to come. Top of the list for dining rooms was a wooden floor, preferably parquet as this was exceptionally hard-wearing. The shelving is multipurpose and flexible enough to accommodate changing storage needs. The white walls avoid changing colour trends and allow the eye to be drawn to the abstract print above the fireplace. Despite the trend for artisan ceramics, throughout the decade, many people still favoured traditional styles.

Right
A venetian blind creates a division between the sitting and dining areas of this dual-purpose 1954 room, although the two spaces are visually linked by the Ercol furniture. The 'Windsor' dining chairs harmonize with the simple lines of the drop-leaf table and spacious sideboard, and a plate-rack used as both storage and a decorative touch. The 'Bergère' easy chairs combine simple design with comfort. Natural motifs are introduced in the sitting area, with a carpet of an interlocking feather design and a Crown wallpaper with a leaf pattern on an off-white ground.

By the Fifties the era of the lavish, formal dinner party had long gone, and the zeitgeist had swung towards a more relaxed approach to entertaining at home. The dining room had already become an endangered species; the new breed of more economically sized houses and flats no longer had the space for a room solely dedicated to dining. Instead, dining areas were frequently incorporated into an area of the kitchen or the sitting room. While the dining room was still a common feature of larger houses, it often retained a more traditional feel than the rest of the Fifties interior. Yet, by looking at the space allocated to dining, it is possible to get an accurate idea of how the house was used as a space for entertaining, as well as for family living.

In the Fifties a dinner-party hostess would normally be expected to prepare the food herself. This made formal meals, with numerous complicated courses served to guests as they sat, very difficult to orchestrate. A simpler style of home cooking prevailed, and dinner parties were typically more relaxed affairs than those enjoyed by previous generations.

The layout of the house began to accommodate this stripped-back approach to entertaining. The kitchen became much more of a social space. If it was large, it could provide a warm and informal place where food could be served as well as prepared. It also had the advantage of not isolating the hostess, and the shorter distance from oven to table made it far easier to serve hot

Below
The furniture in this 1955 dining room is by a now-defunct company named Vesper. The light-blue curtain net is in Terylene, a synthetic material lauded for its durability and ability to wash well without shrinking. The patterned cotton curtains are 'Frobisher' by Fothergay Fabrics. The Crown wallpaper was intended specifically for dining rooms and is in a bold, botanical design of chocolate and two tones of grey. Clashing patterns were often used in the Fifties, and this dining room has clashing colours too, in the brightly coloured lights and the muted upholstery and carpet. The dinner service is a modern Spode design.

Right
Not so much a dining room as a dining alcove, a dedicated eating area fits compactly the corner of this 1954 sitting room. Apple-green walls and mustard carpets seem rather tame beside the bold, floor-to-ceiling curtains in a red-and-green geometric design by Fothergay Fabrics. The Ercol 'Windsor' furniture is a staple of many a Fifties dining area, while some seriously stylish lighting is provided by Troughton & Young, which made the plastic-shaded light over the table and the mahogany, sycamore and brass standard lamp, with its sleek, minimal shade.

food. The advent of the brightly coloured, American-style kitchen had made it a room to be proudly displayed, rather than hidden away like the gloomy basement kitchen of old, which was traditionally the domain of servants. In new builds, the kitchen was usually situated adjacent to a combined sitting and dining area, and serving hatches were common additions. Food could be popped through the hatch for easy transference between kitchen and dining area, although this approach had the unfortunate side effect of making the cook spend much of the evening speaking to her guests through the hatch door, which couldn't have been a particularly enjoyable experience for the hostess. It also meant that it was impossible to effectively keep the smell of cooking out of the sitting area. Today the serving hatch seems like a ridiculously outdated concept, and it is easy to see why it hasn't stood the test of time – open-plan layouts, on the other hand, are even more popular now than they were in the Fifties.

In houses where there was a dining area as opposed to a dining room, it was common to demarcate the area by painting the walls a contrasting colour to the rest of the room. Other ways of making an eating area seem separate might be a different choice of flooring; in larger spaces, a room divider could be used to create a dedicated dining space. Houses that were decorated in a distinctly modern manner might even use metal venetian blinds to divide the room. Dining furniture in these dual-purpose spaces was more likely to be modern, to fit in with the new trends that prevailed in the kitchen and sitting rooms. Furniture

Left

All the furniture in this 1955 dining room is by Ercol. It includes 'Windsor' dining chairs, in an updated version of the 'Windsor' chairs manufactured under the Utility scheme during and just after the Second World War. The oval dining table in elm and beech displays the 'Scroll' range of china by Spode, one of the 'Flemish Green' series. These are in keeping with the curtains, in a mint-green-grey-red-and-black geometric fabric by David Whitehead. The cool colours in the room are warmed up by the sunny yellow walls.

Right

Walls entirely papered in 'No.15158' by Sanderson – featuring a chequered grey-and-yellow leaf motif veined with black – create the starting point for the colours used in this 1954 dining room. The 'Carousel' dining suite is by the British furniture company Gimson & Slater, while the brown-yellow-and-grey carpet was designed by Ronald Grierson for Stockwell. The brass pendant light and table lamp, with its Fornasetti-esque black-and-white shade, are both by Hiscock Appleby.

would probably be made in light-coloured wood, and Ercol's ubiquitous '4A' chair, made in stained-brown beech and elm as part of the Utility scheme, was updated by waxing the wood in a natural colour. Despite being called a kitchen chair, it also became popular as a dining chair, and while it was still an unlikely choice for a formal dining room, it was commonly found in sitting rooms that doubled as an eating area. The gradual spread of Ercol's 'Windsor' chair shows how an increasing practicality

was seeping into interior design, and while patterns on textiles and wallpapers became ever more exuberant and colourful, furniture, in contrast, became simpler and more restrained.

This aesthetic was fundamentally at odds with the traditional concept of the dining room, which was historically decorated in an opulent way. It was a room used for entertaining and for impressing guests. For the houses that retained dining rooms at a time when interiors were undergoing

a major overhaul, it is understandable that the owners often shied away from a modern style of decoration. Regency revival was a popular alternative to modern furniture throughout the decade, and this was particularly well suited to the dining room. This furniture was almost always dark, made of hardwood such as mahogany or walnut, in contrast to the Scandinavian trend for blond wood that was prevalent in modern furniture. Inherited furniture was more likely to end up in the dining room,

Left
Traditional blue-and-white plates add contrast and pattern to this 1952 dining-room set, which manages to incorporate all the primary colours while still retaining a sense of sophistication. The furniture is made by Story, with the dining chairs upholstered in a black-spotted yellow fabric, which contrasts with the bright-red rug. A

black-and-white linoleum floor and a white venetian blind both ensure that this room looks perfectly up to date.

Below
This picture shows Julian Trevelyan and his wife, Mary Fedden, at their home and studio in Chiswick. Both were well-known artists, with work exhibited at the Festival of Britain, and both taught at the Royal College of Art. They were also notable entertainers and often threw dinner parties. As seen here, Mary Fedden typically set the table with white

plates decorated with her own black drawings, enormous shallow bowls of fruit and mixed salads, green goblets and wine glasses. The modern, walnut-handled cutlery shown in this photograph is from Liberty.

and so it often retained a rather dated look, lacking the technological advances that were reshaping the kitchen and the sitting room in the Fifties.

However, even the most determined traditionalist would have been aware of the changing trends in dining. There was a shift away from very formal dining, and buffet-style meals became a popular way of feeding large parties, lessening the pressure on the hostess. This was still no excuse for not decorating the room properly, according to Elizabeth David:

> *'Although the food is cold, have the room warm and looking warm, full of life and colour. If there is no space for flowers, oranges and lemons and apples, arranged with green leaves on small low tables, look every bit as decorative.'*
> —JANUARY 1958

Casserole dishes that could be taken straight from oven to table were popular and gradually found their way from kitchen to dining room, displacing the grand serving tureens of the previous century, which became deeply unfashionable. Artisan pottery was prevalent, while traditional dinner sets were often replaced by china in individual pieces with a linked theme or colour. There was also a vogue for coloured glassware, preferably hand-blown. British porcelain manufacturers such as Wedgwood were still very popular among consumers, and throughout the Fifties the pages of *House & Garden* show that there was still a place for traditional tableware, even if the banquet had been superseded by the buffet.

THE FIFTIES BEDSIT & STUDIO ROOM

'To live happily in one room requires clever planning and great care in the choice of colours used, for the atmosphere produced must suit the varied activities of its owner's life.'

—MARCH 1957

Left
This eye-catching floor may look great, but the tiles are made of vinyl asbestos, marketed in the original 1954 captions as 'the perfect finish'. Still, the deep-pile rug presents far less of a health risk, made of mohair and available in the *House & Garden* colour range. The oak furniture is all by British company Meredew. Much was made of the colourfast properties of the bedlinen, produced by Osman.

Below
In a 1951 preview of the Festival of Britain, this illustration was part of a feature on stylish bedsits for Fifties living. This design was intended for a young bachelor and has a urbane, sophisticated interior suitable for a man-about-town, with the back wall entirely panelled in leather. The divan, by Leslie Mathew, doubles as a bed and a sofa, while the desk and chair are by A J Milne and the armchair is by Howard Keith.

Below
As on page 62, the bedspread on this 1955 divan is from Osman. The popularity of these bedspreads is explained in the accompanying piece: 'a traditional design subtly translated into the mood of the moment. Formalized feathers encircling a small sprigged flower are white; the flower is picked out in bright colours.' The oak furniture is by John and Sylvia Reid

for Stag Furniture, and the upholstered chairs are by Ernest Race. A touch of glamour is added by the Hiscock Appleby brass and mahogany table lamp with a gold-foil shade.

Right
Interior designer Michael Inchbald inherited this house in Chelsea, and he transformed the two attic box rooms into a modern flat that was rented to two business girls. Pictured here in 1954, this house later became the Inchbald School of Design, so it is uncertain how long they retained their elegant quarters. The divan bed shown was used as a sofa by day, and

the low coffee table was adjusted for dining by adding extra sections of leg. The fireplace has been removed and the chimney breast painted the same white as the walls – central heating meant that fireplaces were often taken out during modern conversions, unless deliberately left as a decorative statement.

Today bedsits, or bedsitters, are more commonly known as studio apartments, but the trend for a professional person to occupy a single room that combined sleeping and living areas became particularly popular in the Fifties. This was partly to do with the growing urban population, as an increasing number of young single people flocked to live in the big cities. As such, the bedsit was often the first place a young person would decorate for themselves upon leaving their family home. The rise in the number of professional young women also meant that bedsits were no longer the preserve of men, and the room schemes for bedsits shown in *House & Garden* during the Fifties reflect this. Young, unmarried women had an unprecedented degree of freedom and numerous features aimed at girls decorating their first bedsits seem to unconsciously echo the sentiments of Virginia Woolf on the importance of having 'a room of one's own'. A bedsit was seen as a space where the single woman could express herself, entertain a growing circle of friends and choose a modern style of decoration and colour. It was an exercise in setting up house on a small scale and offered the opportunity to develop individual tastes and to accumulate key pieces of furniture that could be relocated to a larger home in the future.

The magazine made a point of running a feature on how to decorate a bedsit in its preview of the 1951 Festival of Britain. It also showed the diverse ages of the people who might occupy them – everyone from teenagers to the elderly. In the festival, designer John Dawson Binns presented four different bedsits, each aimed at a very different occupant. The first room, intended

Left
Colourful textiles liven up this 1957 bedsit, which was designed for a teenage girl. The Welsh wool tapestry quilt is from Brynkir weavers John Jones & Son, while the brightly patterned patchwork throw is handmade. The ladder-back chairs and the table are by Meredew and could be used for dining or for study. A His Master's Voice gramophone and a cork pinboard add to the youthful, expressive feel of this economically furnished space.

for two 14-year-old boys, had double bunks and space for making things; the second was for a teenage girl and had clothes storage under the sofa bed, to prevent it from looking too much like a bedroom when she entertained; the third catered for a bachelor and had a sofa bed, a shower unit and basin; while the fourth was for an old lady and her cat, and was fitted with a gas ring, hidden away in a cabinet, so that she could 'make tea tidily, amid homely antiques'.

What is so interesting about the bedsit is that it provides a microcosm of an entire house in a single room. As space is limited,

the design has to be functional and the layout needs careful consideration in order to avoid clutter. A major difference between modern studios and their Fifties counterparts is that, in the latter, great effort was taken to conceal the functional elements of the room – clothes, sleeping areas and any food-preparation areas were carefully hidden away when not in use. In particular, great pains were taken to conceal the presence of the bed. Whether it was a screen, a bed that could be folded against the wall or a sofa bed (in the Fifties these were called a 'divan'

or a 'bed-settee', depending on the style), there was a real determination to make a distinction between day and night, sitting and sleeping. The modern studio often has a double bed, which may still be screened off, or at a mezzanine level, though more commonly left in full view, whereas in the Fifties a single, folding bed was the most popular sleeping option. How to take the bed out of the bedsit was a common dilemma of interior design, and many furniture companies created innovative, if uncomfortable-looking, solutions.

Because living in a bedsit nearly always

Right
This 1959 bedsit was designed for a music
student with a penchant for modern design.
The sofa at the end of the room could be
transformed into a bed; the cupboard at the
right fulfilled the purpose of a bedside table.
A stylish teak coffee table from Heal's could
be transformed into a dining table thanks to
its adjustable legs. Heal's also supplied the
Danish oak-frame chairs, with leather arms
and suede seat pads. This clever design even
leaves room for a piano – or at least a spinet.
This one is by Arnold Dolmetsch.

equated to having a limited income, it
made sense that suggested interiors for
these spaces were economical. Bedsits were
usually for the young setting up a home for
the first time, who were keen to adopt new
trends as well as decorating on a budget.
Contemporary patterns were popular and
so were bright paint colours. Although
traditional patterns such as Victorian
sprigs and Regency stripes and medallions
also had a following, especially during the
early Fifties, by the end of the decade the
contemporary had won out and had become
the prevailing style.

As well as a space for young professionals
and the elderly, the bedsit has also
traditionally been the preserve of the
student. Many ideas for bedsit decoration
incorporate study areas, in which desks take
priority. In some cases, the bedsit was taken
as a model for decorating the bedroom
of an older child in the family home; for
a teenager studying for exams, the bedsit
model provided a space that could double as
a study, while also reflecting their individual
tastes and providing them with some much-
needed privacy.

Left
This design for a boy's room was displayed at Heal's in 1953. The tubular-steel bunk beds were designed by Christopher Heal, who had been made design director of Heal's the previous year. The wicker-seated stools and the rocking chair are by Terence Conran and were stocked by Heal's, which also stocked the Swedish rug and the 'Small Hours' printed curtain fabric. The colourful yet highly practical decoration of this room allowed it to function as a proper living space as opposed to simply a place to sleep.

Above
Purple-upholstered furniture from Hille – tub chairs, a sofa bed and a 'Hilleon' chair – creates a stylish scheme in this 1957 bedsit. This room has a sophisticated and studious atmosphere, with a plain moss-green carpet and walls painted in white and green. An Anglepoise lamp sits on the Finmar desk, while the series of photographs of the Elgin Marbles displayed on the wall continues the scholarly theme.

Below

In this 1957 bedsit, the emphasis is on entertaining, as the empty wine bottles would suggest. The hand-printed cerulean-and-grey wallpaper is from Sanderson, while the furniture is Scandinavian in style and includes a cane armchair designed by Finn Juhl and a dressing table and sheepskin-covered stool from Stag.

Right

A Japanese influence informed certain design trends of the mid-Fifties, as can be seen in this 1956 bedsit. The bed is a low 'safari bed', from the Army & Navy Stores: it had the same understated effect as a futon and could be folded away when not in use. Painted furniture, in this case the rustic-style chairs, adds colour to a very economically furnished space, with white walls, 'Geebro Cord' floor covering and a generously proportioned window – inexplicably featuring a window cleaner.

'HOW TO READ FOR AN HONOURS DEGREE IN COMFORTABLE SELF-CONTAINMENT'

OCTOBER 1959

While a bedsit functioned as a private space for younger teenagers within the family home, university students had to create not just a study but a proper self-sufficient space, though simple bedsits often came pre-furnished if they were part of university accommodation. The following pages show a feature that House & Garden *ran on interior design in university rooms, in which it presented advice on how to create a bedsit that any undergraduate would be proud to live in. The feature provides a unique insight into how rooms at Oxford and Cambridge were decorated.*

Above
Behind the 17th-century façade of this 1959 bedsit in Corpus Christi, Oxford, is a surprisingly modern room with functional furniture and a red Anglepoise lamp for studying by. A green wall provides a bold shot of colour in an otherwise neutral space.

Right
With its clever shelving unit providing ample storage for books, svelte, black-legged furniture and abstract rugs covering the dark floorboards, this room was captioned 'the most uncompromisingly modern, clear-cut room in the University'. It belonged to David Butler, who has been a Fellow of Nuffield since 1951 and is the author of many highly regarded books on politics.

Above
'Books, books and more books dominate these Oxford rooms' reads the original caption to this 1959 feature on the accommodation of students.

Above left
In Oxford, brilliant primary colours and decorative motifs from the Far East add an exotic atmosphere to the Holywell flat of anthropologist Ronald Needham and his wife. The powder-pink walls balance well with the rich blue carpet. Paper lampshades were popular during the Fifties, but these decorative ones add to the Asian influence in this flat.

Left
Undergraduates unwind in a modern block of student housing in Clare College, Cambridge.

Below
Immediately after the extended feature on the interiors of the world's two oldest universities, *House & Garden* suggested its own design for an undergraduate's bedsit, allowing for sleeping, entertaining and studying. A divan can be concealed as a sofa if desired, while the modern desk and cupboard units were designed by the architectural firm Yorke, Rosenberg and Mardall and made by Bath Cabinet Makers. The birch table is an Aalto-Artek design; the shelving along the left-hand wall could be adjusted as required; and the rush matting was from Heal's. Two Anglepoise lamps, the black '1227a' on the desk and a cream '1209' on the table, provide focused lighting.

'The magazine visited the world's oldest universities, to see how undergraduates live in their converted medieval quarters and, occasionally in recently built bed-sitters. They also visited amenable dons.

'The discomforts of Oxford and Cambridge colleges are legendary and, unlike most legends, well authenticated. The most vociferous denigrators are neither Fellows nor undergraduates, but businessmen-planners quartered in the colleges for summer schools and conferences. A wartime naval officer, temporarily housed in Hertford College, Oxford, begged to be allowed to return to the amenities of his cabin in a warship in the North Atlantic. Most colleges are afraid of colour and modern design. That is the real trouble, despite the fact that there are Common or Combination Rooms at both Oxford and Cambridge which are quite certainly of our own time. Lincoln College, Oxford, has a Common Room which has been described by one don, with an air of disapproval, as being indistinguishable from the waiting room of a small, rather exclusive airport. Another trouble is that the decorating of college rooms is decided by Committee. In one college, it is alleged, the Committee appointed to deal with lighting for the Hall in 1912 has just been reappointed – to a man – to renew that lighting. It is also true that the efforts towards enlivening the decoration of undergraduates' rooms do not always meet with the success they deserve. Agglomerations of eight weeks' non-washing up will mar the best-laid scheme.

'College furniture is usually basic or hideous or both. Of course college furniture has to last – but need it be so unyieldingly obnoxious? Especially the three-piece suites. Occasionally, bachelor dons can afford to lavish time and cash on furnishing and redecorating, rooting out good bits of college furniture and dusty, deep-stored college pictures. (One Fellow found and hung with pride a very large-scale picture of Joseph and Potiphar's wife, with the peculiar aim, it is said, of embarrassing his female pupils.) More forceful dons can and do persuade their colleges into the use of colour.

'More time and trouble is now spent on housing and cosseting undergraduates than at any time in the universities' long history. In the newer buildings there has been a return to what Christopher Hobhouse called the 'medieval simplicity of the hateful bed-sitter'. But beautiful rooms suffer from an undergraduate lack of time and money. Many undergraduates now spend only one year in college and few can afford to redecorate their rooms on that fleeting basis. While the unimpeded reconstructions of the exteriors continues, and new colleges are built, influxes of fresh undergraduates and Fellows will have the opportunity of taking over some of the most attractive and challenging rooms in the world as well as some of the least promising. Is it too much to hope that in time the interiors may come to match the impact of the architecture? Cream and brown are not a legacy that should be passed on.'

THE FIFTIES BEDROOM

'Create a serene setting to induce sleep as invigorating as any bottled tonic.'

—SEPTEMBER 1955

Above left
A sprigged floral Crown wallpaper compliments the chintz Lister curtains. Everwear candlewick bedspreads were popular and in this 1952 scheme a pink version is shown alongside lavender 'Dunswayne' bedlinen (colourfast, synthetic bedlinen led to a trend for brightly coloured sheets). The furniture, which has a two-tone effect thanks to the contrasting woods, is from Finewood.

Above right
Blue tones create a restful scheme in this 1953 room. Along with the cameos beside the headboard, a bold Sanderson wallpaper in a Jacobean-inspired design adds a feminine touch to the room, which has simple oak Meredew furniture. The powder-blue Sunway venetian blind is offset by the yellow mohair Field's rug and the stool upholstered in a similar textured fabric to the curtains.

Right
In a 1954 room, the layered carpet is broken up by a pair of 'Viceroy' rugs designed for Stockwell by Ronald Grierson. The 'Cumberland' bedroom furniture, by John and Sylvia Reid, is from Stag and comprises a dressing table, a four-drawer chest and a wardrobe with a full-length mirror. The deep red wall matches the shade on the Troughton & Young ceramic table lamp.

Left
Sunway venetian blinds were manufactured in a wide range of colours, including yellow, seen here in this 1955 child's room. Below the dado, the wall has been painted in blackboard paint, to provide a generous space for drawing, while a mural has been drawn above it. The red triangle emphasizes the room's vertical space, while at the same time being in keeping with the child-friendly decoration. The blackboard-topped table and child-size modern chairs are from Heal's, as is the tubular-metal shelving unit.

Below
Gold-and-navy carpeting creates dramatic colour blocking in this 1958 child's bedroom. A Fraser 'Long John' bunk bed, shown here in oak, but also made in mahogany, comes complete with a 'Davy Jones' Locker', which provides storage underneath the bed. Continuing the theme of unusual names, the mahogany magazine rack is from Fyne Lady Furniture. This company also made the mahogany bench that could double as an occasional table and is here used in place of a bedside table. A two-arm table lamp from Forrest Modern Light Fittings adds to the functional yet playful atmosphere.

There were three features that characterized the Fifties bedroom. The most obvious of these was the use of colour, particularly on the walls. Bold tones were often used in bedrooms, as in the rest of the house: typically, one wall would be papered with a bold print, while the other walls would be painted in a strong shade. No single colour dominated these schemes, but shades included red, plum, yellow and blue. Even the more subtle schemes were far from neutral – pinks and lilacs might be used for a fresher, more feminine interior. The second characteristic that distinguished the Fifties bedroom from its Forties counterpart was that it was usually carpeted – fitted carpets were by far the most popular flooring choice for bedrooms. It created a feeling of warmth and luxury; a necessary touch when you consider that the newly installed central heating would rarely have extended as far as the bedroom.

The third thing that gave the Fifties bedroom its distinctive appearance was the penchant for matching furniture – the bedside table was usually in a similar style to the bed, and even the wardrobe and dressing table might be of a matching design. This look grew partly out of the standard-issue Utility furniture that was the only type of new furniture available in Britain throughout the Forties and up until 1952. The initial, limited range offered barely any choice, while the later, expanded Utility catalogues had two collections, the 'Chiltern' and the 'Cotswold'. Each offered a couple of different models of beds, dressing tables, wardrobes and occasional tables. As new homeowners had to choose from this range if they didn't inherit any furniture,

Below
The ever-present Everwear candlewick bedspread appears again in a 1953 bedroom, this time in a grey-on-white pattern, as does the popular Field's deep-pile mohair rug in a pale pink. The chest of drawers, dressing table, stool and bedside cupboards are all by Hille and made of agba (a tropical hardwood) and walnut. The oil painting above the bed is

by Jan Wieliczko – a Polish artist who had settled in Britain – while the black monotype is by British artist Russell Quay. The multi-legged 'Kalyx' table lamps are from Hiscock Appleby.

Right
This 1955 scheme features bedroom furniture by Meredew, veneered in French walnut. This time, the Everwear 'Hobnail' candlewick bedspread is decorated with no fewer than 4,000 pompoms. Crossley's Wilton carpet has an unusual pattern called 'Mayan Dogs', which was inspired by the abstract designs that were so popular in

furnishing fabrics. The printed-cotton curtain fabric is 'Richmond', by Fothergay Fabrics. Even a relatively restrained Fifties scheme such as this one still incorporates an expansive colour palette – background details such as the net curtains are coloured, in this instance, in a pale blue.

the fitted look originated out of necessity rather than aesthetic preference. Even after the restrictions on furniture design were lifted, the taste for matching bedroom furniture remained and a desire for matching continued throughout the decade, even though the designs and materials used altered – metal became a popular alternative to wood and was used for bed frames and side tables.

The colourful appearance of the Fifties bedroom was also created by the use of textiles. Curtains were often brightly patterned and there was a prevailing taste for brightly coloured bed linen, which was increasingly available in synthetic fabrics, then considered to be a novel and exciting development. *House & Garden* recorded the latest fashions in bedding, which tended towards striped, printed and embroidered

sheets in cheerful colours. Readers were also encouraged to stick to a more classic look – white linen never went out of fashion, and could be given a fresh look when used with strong-coloured blankets. Fitted sheets in white nylon were also advocated; they were seen as convenient in houses that had a constant passage of guests. Terylene pillows were considered chic and contemporary, and had the benefits of being soft, resilient

and long-lasting. The fact that they could be washed easily – unlike their feather counterparts – and were suitable for those with allergies, meant that these became a popular alternative to down pillows.

The main bedroom was seen as a personal sanctuary, which could be decorated in a characterful way and displayed the occupants' own taste. It was seen as the ideal place to display favourite pieces of art, treasured collections and books. By contrast, the spare room was usually decorated in a less personal way and, just as the kitchen might now also act as a dining area, so houses with limited space might combine the function of a spare room, so it could double as a study or as an extra living space when there were no house guests. Desks that could double as dressing tables were popular, as their adaptable design worked well in a space that needed to be flexible. Advice on the bed situation was conflicted; at one end of the spectrum, there was the suggestion of installing a sofa bed that could be sat on during the day and slept on at night, if space was too limited to comfortably accommodate a full-sized bed. A more hospitable approach advised that the comfort of guests came first; *House & Garden* advocated a completely empty wardrobe, comfortable mattress, fresh linen and flowers. The same article also suggested leaving a carton of the guest's favourite brand of cigarettes on the bedside table, although it is doubtful whether that particular suggestion will be taken up by many present-day hosts.

Attention was also given to children's rooms. Decoration was often fun and informal, and colour schemes were bright.

Above
A Cole & Son paper in a harlequin pattern decorates a wall of this 1955 girl's bedroom. As the adjoining wall is painted a deep plum and the carpet is deep grey, these darker colours offset the pink and lend the scheme an air of sophistication. The bed, table, lamp and carpet are from Harrods, while the picture and the slim glass vase, almost invisible behind the glass decanter from Harrods, are both from Liberty.

Right
A bed covered in red-and-white ticking and a wall lamp from Heal's add a smart note to this masculine 1955 bedroom. With the exception of the picture and the ashtray, everything in this room is from Heal's, which exemplified modern, stylish design during the Fifties. This room has a simple, masculine design without being sparse, decorative interest being added by the bold colour scheme.

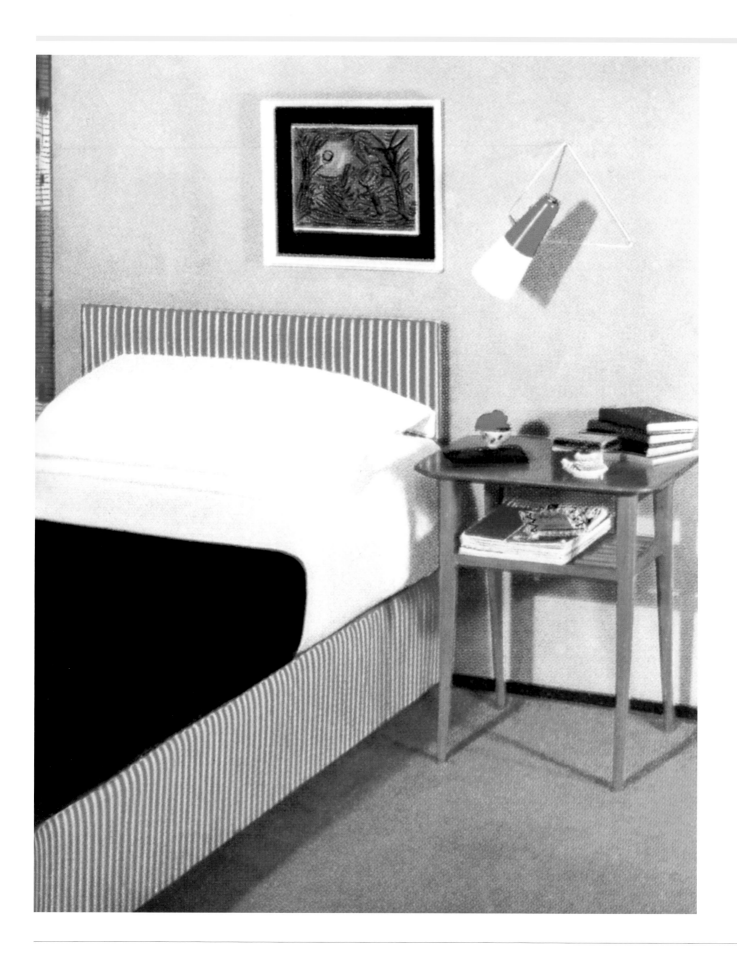

Left

Rich, autumnal colours decorate this 1954 bedroom, with a deep-red carpet and a Crown wallpaper in a bold leaf print. A clashing pattern is provided by the curtains, in a heavyweight Fothergay cotton. Gimson & Slater bedroom furniture, with mahogany interiors and exteriors veneered in French walnut, adds to the rustic colours of this room, as does the set of green-and-white tableware from Heal's. An oil heater from Harper's stands in the centre of the room – an example of the ever-more sophisticated forms of heating that were appearing on the market.

Below

Strong colours create a room suitable for a stylish bachelor. The bed is a Meyer divan with a 'Matchmaker' headboard. Although the presence of an ashtray on the bedside table suggests that this room clearly belonged to an adult, the single bed revealed that, in 1955, bachelor flats were certainly not furnished with cohabitation in mind.

However, the Fifties emphasis on economy meant that the primary consideration when designing a child's room was adaptability, so that the same furniture could accommodate the changing needs of a growing child; for example, shelving used to display a child's toys could be used to store books when the child became older. While nursery designs included a measure of comfort for adults as well as babies, great importance was placed on ensuring that rooms for older toddlers and children were thoughtfully tailored to their occupants. *House & Garden* wrote:

'Use imagination in decoration, for your children are going to remember for the rest of their lives the visual surroundings of their most formative years, and it's your responsibility towards them to make these as pleasant as possible. Children will gaze for hours at the pictures on their walls and travel with them far into the realms of fantasy, so see that the standard of drawings, paintings or prints on the nursery walls is the very highest possible. They can't learn everything at school; home is the standard by which they will judge the world.'

—SEPTEMBER 1955

It emphasized the importance on the bedroom as a showcase of personal taste. In an adult's room, favourite objects could be grouped together to create a haven, while a child's room fostered the developing taste of its occupant. Bright colours teamed with the clean lines of modern furniture were in vogue for children and adults alike, helping to establish the Fifties bedroom as a vibrant yet intimate space.

Left

This 1957 room was decorated in colours chosen from that year's *House & Garden* range. The curtains are in a 'Lilac Denim'; the floor is in 'Hollyhock', and there is a 'Citron' base on the 'Palladio' wallpaper from Wall Paper Manufacturers. This scheme was intended for a young girl, so the dual-purpose dressing table and desk from Hille makes the most of limited space. The cane and metal chair is from Hiscock Appleby.

Below left

A pillow fight takes places in very stylish surroundings in this 1955 children's room. A Cole & Son wallpaper, 'Le Kiosque à Musique', creates a lively atmosphere, while modern touches include the Sunway venetian blind, linoleum floor and a cane chair from Conran Furniture. The 'Jason' chair was designed by Carl Jacobs but was made by British firm Kandya, who also made the Wareite-topped table beside it.

Right

The wallpaper's three-dimensional block design, on a grey ground, breaks up the flat area of the walls' surfaces. A complex effect has been created with the window dressing: a black curtain with its bright floral design adds colour to the room, while a grass-green net curtain softens the effect of the venetian blind. The wall-mounted lamp and the table lamp, both from Hiscock Appleby, illuminate the textured effect. The furniture was designed by Ward & Austin for Loughborough Furniture.

Above
Pink-and-white striped wallpaper from Cole & Son is used with sophistication in this 1957 bedroom; the dramatic stripes are neutralized by the dark grey of the wall below the dado. Extra drama is created by the black-and-white 'Fools' linen, designed by Cecil Collins for Edinburgh Weavers. The furniture is all by British companies and includes a dressing chest from Gomme and an upholstered G Plan stool. The 'Sugar Scoop' chair by the bed is by G W Scott & Sons.

Above
'Boys need workshops' read the original article that accompanied this 1955 photograph. This bedroom, designed for a young teenage boy, is just that, with practical furniture and even a space on the wall to hang tools. A rush mat is a robust choice of flooring, while furniture is modern and simple, and includes Conran Furniture's 'Tripolina' chair and a stacking chair from Hille. A Finmar stick chair provides seating at a Herbert Berry desk. The entire room is a triumph of unfussy, modern design that is tailored to its occupant.

THE FIFTIES BATHROOM

'The days of the nondescript bathroom are over. New shapes and new equipment demand new backgrounds; to the economical planning of space are added all the excitements of colour, pattern and texture. When you begin to consider your bathroom as a room in its own right you will become aware of its many possibilities – you can use it as a dressing room, thus eliminating wardrobes from the bedroom; or for exercising if you have enough floor area. Only one word of warning – don't make your bathroom so comfortable and luxurious that you never use your living room.'

—JULY 1955

Left
A 1954 feature on bathrooms included this elegant example from a London town house. Three tones of green are used in this design: sage green on a wall; emerald green for the carpet and for the protective panel of glass that is used instead of tiles above the bath; and a grey-green in the Scandinavian botanical-print wallpaper. The Italian wall brackets that support terracotta pots of ivy continue the botanical theme of this room.

Above
This 1959 children's bathroom has a simple yet playful design that is very modern. A lively wallpaper – 'Joanna' from the 'Palladio' collection – adds interest to the wall, as does the bright-red ceiling. Simple white tiles and a venetian blind stop this room from looking too fussy, as does the simple curve of the 'Marnoc' wall-mounted basin. A lime-green door adds the final shot of colour to this highly effective scheme.

Left
Grey-and-brown chequered floor tiles and teal walls create a dramatic effect in this 1958 bathroom. The bath, by Radiation, has corner taps, designed to be easier to reach. Above is an adjustable twin wall light from Hiscock Appleby. The 'TX49' table lamp is from the same company, and was specially wired to prevent potential water-related mishaps.

Below
Different shades of blue combine to create a fresh, bright bathroom in 1958. The floor is in cornflower linoleum, while the bath and the basin are both blue, from Allied Ironfounders. In the foreground is a blue-and-white towelling curtain in a rose design by G P & J Baker, the plastic and chromium stool is from Tylors on Tottenham Court Road, while the Italian

screen is by Fornasetti. The towels are from John Lewis, while the collection of French glass bottles are antiques.

Although it was unlikely that many people adopted the advice on the previous page and turned their bathrooms into a wardrobe-cum-gym – engaging though the idea is – the Fifties saw a revolution in bathroom design. At the most basic level, having a bathroom inside the house was still regarded as being a luxury in itself. Before the Fifties, internal bathrooms might not have existed at all in some houses – for many people, bathing had been considered a weekly chore involving a tin bath, while going to the lavatory meant a trip to a shed outside the house. In densely populated, less-affluent urban areas, these outdoor lavatories would have been shared between neighbours. In the Fifties, for the first time, people of all classes were able to have an indoor bathroom, and a surge of interest in bathroom furnishings reflected this rapidly expanding market.

Stylistically, the bathroom was a work in progress throughout the decade. Many houses had a bathroom with a separate lavatory, which was placed in a small adjacent room. Britain still lagged behind the States, which had already started installing en-suite bathrooms – an idea inspired by hotel design.

In general, bathrooms haven't changed much since the Fifties. Then, as now, the typical bathroom consisted of a matching three-piece suite of lavatory, basin and bath. The difference is that there was far more deliberation about the design of these during the Fifties than there is today. Although Scandinavia and Italy were early adopters of modern bathroom fittings, in Britain, clunky design persisted until the latter years of the decade, but when these international influences began to seep into

the design aesthetic, it opened up an array of new possibilities.

Previously, bathroom fittings had been rather cumbersome and square-cut, but as the Fifties progressed a trend emerged for flowing lines rather than sharp angles and ridges. These pared-back designs had the added advantage of being much cheaper to produce than the old, bulkier shapes, and they also took up less space. Basins were

Below
Bathrooms went from being one of the most neglected rooms of the house to one of the most considered, as can be seen from a December 1959 *House & Garden* feature that presented stylish ideas for bathroom design. The clever design of this bathroom was thought up by a fellow of the Royal British Association of Architects, Brian Peake. Along with the

built-in basin, the cistern of this lavatory is completely concealed within the curving, Formica-covered unit.

Right
A large floral-patterned wallpaper covers both walls and ceiling of this 1959 bathroom. There is even a matching shower curtain. A simple colour palette creates a smart effect, with matching blue storage containers, stool and table lamp, and wood painted in black gloss paint. Opulence is created by the deep-pile white carpet.

often hung on brackets instead of pedestals – another space-saving idea – or else were set into sheets of marble, mosaic or plastic, with fitted units beneath.

Apart from the basic bathroom fittings, further decoration was encouraged to stop the room appearing dull and clinical. Bathing had become an enjoyable experience, and one to be undertaken in pleasant rather than spartan surroundings. Magazine articles suggested ways of injecting character into what was traditionally a cold and faceless room. Colourful or floral wallpaper was a popular way to brighten up a bathroom; walls were decorated with framed pictures; and plants added life and character to what could otherwise be a slightly sterile space.

Wallpapers could either be varnished for a waterproof finish or bought pre-treated; Sanderson and Cole & Son both offered a range of washable wallpapers, or the option to add a waterproof finish to any of their existing papers, which meant that there was suddenly an unprecedented array of simple, practical options for decorating bathroom walls. Oil-bound distemper was considered better than gloss paint, as it had a more porous surface and would temporarily absorb the moisture in the air instead of letting it trickle down the walls in rivulets.

Flooring, too, underwent a makeover. Underfloor heating made a variety of different bathroom floors possible; previously chilly options, such as marble flags or ceramic and glass mosaics, often of Swedish or Italian design, could now be used. Floorboards were usually covered up with linoleum or with one of the plastic or rubber floor finishes that were widely

Left

Ribbed glass has been used in the sliding doors above these twin basins to easily see the toiletries stored behind them (*top left*). This bathroom counter is of black marble inlaid with mother-of-pearl (*top centre*). Floor-to-ceiling tiles create a modern look (*top right*). Patterned curtains from Edinburgh Weavers enliven a child's bathroom (*centre left*). The metal frame that supports this black terrazzo bathroom counter doubles as a towel rail (*centre*). Ahead of its time: a small bathroom has a shower unit instead of a bath (*centre right*). Textured tiles decorate a shower unit (*bottom left*). Sanderson waterproof wallpaper adds colour and luxury (*bottom centre*). Plate glass protects wallpaper from water damage (*bottom right*). All pictures from 1959.

Right

In a 1956 feature on how to add individuality to bathrooms, it was suggested to decorate them in a manner similar to any other room in the house. Here, mirrored shelving displays a collection of ornaments and glass bottles, while floral curtains and an antique chair complement the high ceilings of this period property.

available. These were popular as they could be bought in bright colours and were very durable. Cork tiles were also commonly used for bathroom floors as they were cheap and warm underfoot.

Heated towel rails became an affordable indulgence – oil-powered central heating made these easy to install – while extractor fans meant that bathrooms could be ventilated without having to open a window. Extractor fans also prompted a change in building regulations – bathrooms with no natural daylight were allowed provided that they had adequate ventilation. The number of dingy, windowless bathrooms across Britain today can be traced back to

this decade. Shower cabinets also started to appear as a space-saving alternative to the bath. Oddly, these were advertised as being a useful, movable device that could be taken with you if you moved house. Showers were self-contained cabinets, which had a shower tray, waterproof walls and shower curtains. Although they had to be installed by a plumber, shower cabinets, much like white goods in the kitchen, were seen in the Fifties as being the property of the owner, rather than as a standard, immovable item found in all rental properties.

This new interest in bathroom design had originated in the States, which was the first to modernize this neglected room.

During the Fifties the bathroom underwent a Cinderella-style transformation from functionality to luxury. Better heating and a new attention to decoration transformed it into a pleasant room to spend time in. Toiletries began to move out of the bedroom and on to the new basin units. The bathroom became a space to bathe, dress, shave or apply make-up in – in some cases, twin 'his 'n' hers' basins were installed. This new attitude towards (formerly) the most humble room in the house was best summarized in a *House & Garden* feature from December 1959, which concluded: 'A bathroom is a place to restore your morale, as well as your looks.'

Below

The phoenix mosaic mural certainly enlivens this 1958 bathroom. A plain white bath and a floating bathroom cabinet with sliding doors give the mosaic centre stage. It was made by the artist and *Punch* cartoonist Brian Robb, who also taught at the Chelsea School of Art, and designed posters and advertisements for Shell and London Underground.

Below
This 1954 bathroom was part of a bachelor pad. Textured, petrol-blue glass panels cover the walls, while the bath and its buttoned-pleather panelling are in ice blue. The aqueous scheme is brightened by the red floor tiles and towels. The ceiling, although it is not visible here, is covered in wallpaper with a narrow blue-and-white stripe.

British actress Adrianne Allen owned this amply decorated bathroom, shown here in 1955. The American floral wallpaper forms the basis for the scheme; its pink geraniums, with their abundant green foliage, inform the colour of the grass-green woodwork. A mirrored wall behind the bath creates a feeling of spaciousness in a relatively small room.

Below
A 1955 feature illustrated how to use storage and decorative details in different ways, depending on the size of the room. A large bathroom (*below*) is partially divided by a useful storage wall, while the gilded mirror over the dressing table adds a touch of opulence. In a smaller bathroom (*bottom*), cabinets are fitted over the bath, and a painted cupboard is used for the main storage. A fitted mirror over the dressing table helps to give the illusion of space.

Below right
Two large, ornate gilt mirrors, their frames made to appear even richer by the dark-green walls behind them, reflect each other and give depth to this small 1954 bathroom in London. A white bath, chair and carpet, and a delicate, ivy-patterned fabric, lighten the scheme.

Below

This dressing alcove opens off the large, bathroom shown on page 103. The images were taken from a 1958 feature, 'Beauty and the Bath', which took the bathing habits of ancient Rome and the most lavish contemporary designs from the United States as inspiration for how to create a really sumptuous bathroom. The pink walls and gold lights suggest a luxury worthy of any Hollywood screen siren. Another smart decorative touch is the array of monogrammed towels, the sheer abundance of which means that they have a visual impact as well as a practical function.

Below
While the dressing alcove is prettily pink, the bathroom itself takes classical Rome as its influence. A mural on the wall makes the decorative reference crystal clear and is supplemented by the sunken, tiled bath, day bed and elegantly draped fabric – classical decadence reinterpreted for the United States of the 1950s.

2. HOUSES

138
'DESIGNERS AT HOME'

CASE STUDY | JANUARY 1954

150
'THE BRIGHTER LOOK'

CASE STUDY | MARCH 1956

162
'ARTIST IN RESIDENCE'

CASE STUDY | OCTOBER 1958

142
'A NEW LEASE'

CASE STUDY | SEPTEMBER 1954

154
'IT BEGAN WITH TWO MUD HUTS'

CASE STUDY | DECEMBER 1956

168
'THE HOUSE WITH FOLDING WALLS'

CASE STUDY | APRIL 1959

146
'SMALL HOUSE IN HAMPSTEAD'

CASE STUDY | NOVEMBER 1955

158
'SETTING UP HOUSE THE HARD WAY'

CASE STUDY | JUNE 1957

172
'MODERN MASTERPIECE'

CASE STUDY | NOVEMBER 1959

THE 'HOUSE OF IDEAS'

While Part One of this book looked at how individual rooms might have been decorated during the Fifties, this part takes a more general view of the house as a whole. As a magazine, House & Garden *was very conscious of the relationship between architecture and interior design; historically, the two have always been linked. Architects such as John Soane and James Wyatt also designed the interiors of the great houses that they built. By the Fifties, interior design had emerged as a separate entity, but there was nevertheless a desire to have a house that was planned for modern living, inside and out. Over two consecutive years, the magazine twice outlined a 'House of Ideas' – a modern house tailored to its occupants, from foundations to furniture. The sheer ambition of these two projects has resulted in a pair of prototypes of the ideal Fifties house, outlined in incredible detail. More than anything else, these houses show what the Fifties dream really was – two imagined houses that encompassed the ideals, values and fashions of an era.*

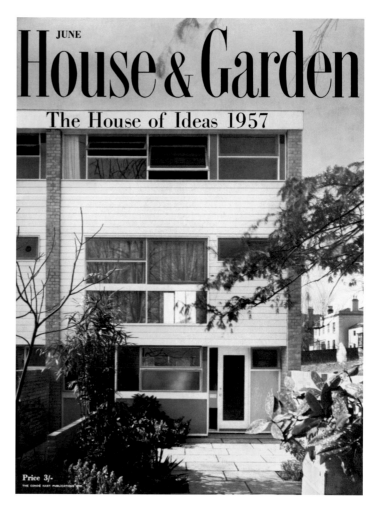

Above
The second 'House of Ideas', a terrace house, catered for urban living and was shown in June and July 1957.

Right
The results of both 'Houses of Ideas' were each shown across two issues. The first 'House of Ideas' was designed for rural or suburban living and ran in the September and October 1956 issues.

SEPTEMBER

House & Garden

The House of Ideas

Price 3/-
THE CONDÉ NAST PUBLICATIONS LTD.

'COUNTRY LIVING ON STILTS'

'HOUSE OF IDEAS' | 1956

In 1956 House & Garden *commissioned the architect Kenneth Capon (who subsequently designed the University of Essex) to produce a model of the perfect modern house. His brief was to create a home for a couple with two children, living in the country or the outskirts of a town. He envisaged a timber house, set up on posts for privacy and to make the most of the view, with a raised sun deck running around the perimeter. It was planned as a series of fully heated, linked rooms without any corridor space, and with a 9m (30ft) living room at the south end of the house. Floor-to-ceiling glass windows, with French windows that opened on to the sun deck, created a light-filled interior. Although this plan was a prototype for the magazine, the architect built his own house in West Sussex to a very similar plan.*

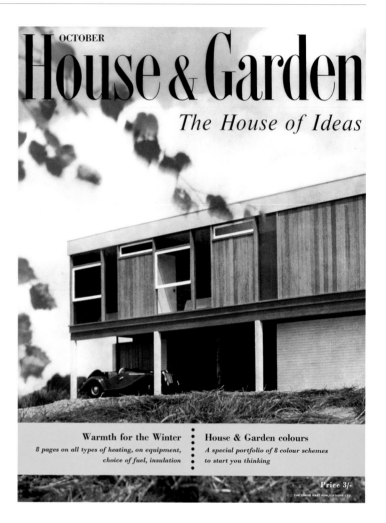

Right
The partitions that divide up the rooms of the 1956 house were movable, so the internal layout could be adjusted to suit the occupants, removing partitions to allow for fewer bedrooms, or to create an open-plan living space. The floor-to-ceiling windows allowed for a huge amount of natural light. Underfloor heating was an unobtrusive and modern way of heating the house.

Left
As the house was of such a futuristic design, the furniture was deliberately chosen to be homely and eclectic rather than resolutely modern to provide a contrast. It was designed with a young couple in mind, and the furniture would have been a mix of new and inherited or borrowed pieces. The wood-panelled partition walls were simple to remove if the internal space of the house needed to be reconfigured.

Below
This shows an alternative angle of the living area pictured opposite. As the house had no attic, concealed storage was built into the design of the rooms, and modern wood and metal shelving provided a place to display ornaments and artwork. The coffee tables are by Conran Furniture.

Ground floor

The main living space of the house was raised off the ground for practical as well as aesthetic reasons. It let in more sunshine and provided a better outlook. It lifted the house away from damp and insects if the site was marshy or surrounded by trees, and in built-up suburban areas it gave a greater sense of security and seclusion. Also, the surroundings of the house were freed from the untidiness of outbuildings, as a large area of covered storage space was provided that could be later developed into further rooms without too much expense or inconvenience to the family living on the floor above. There were other less tangible but important architectural reasons for raising the house in this way. The site is not broken up, it keeps its character and, as a result, a small site appears larger.

Below
The design of the house incorporated a generous terrace, raised like the rest of the building to make the most of the sun. This outdoor sun deck could be used as a playroom and extra sitting room, as well as a secluded place for sunbathing or as an additional area for dining, as it opened on to the kitchen (as shown in the picture opposite) as well as the living area.

Right
The French windows ensure that the kitchen is flooded with natural light. The wrap-around kitchen units neatly house all the appliances, including refrigerator, cooker and three sinks (one fitted with a Wastemaster). A metal-framed island unit – comprising a worktop with shelves above it – is disguised by a mosaic backing by Robyn Denny.

Kitchen

For ease of cleaning and to establish a sense of order – very necessary in a kitchen exposed to view from the rest of the house – a terrazzo work surface ran unbroken round the room. To achieve this, a refrigerator and waist-high oven were grouped together in a central island. At the north end of the kitchen was the food storage area – dry goods were kept in cupboards over the preparation counter, vegetables in ventilated racks below and the large refrigerator just behind in the island unit. Below the sink were cupboards for cooking equipment. Directly below the serving hatch was a smaller refrigerator for food used solely in the dining room and a cupboard for food that needed no preparation before serving. There were three sinks: the first was fitted with a Wastemaster, which could churn most waste to liquid for disposal through an ordinary waste pipe, the second sink was for washing-up and the third was for rinsing.

Below
Natural tones dominate the main
bedroom. The dressing-desk –
particularly popular during the Fifties for
its versatility – is made of mahogany and
is by Hille, while the black 'Chiavari' chair
is from Conran Furniture. A bearskin rug
covers the floor.

Main bedroom

On the other side of the sun deck, opposite
the kitchen, was the main bedroom.
Planned, basically, as a cul-de-sac off the
study, this was the only room without a
possible dual purpose, and the quietest
corner of the house. Its arrangement was
traditional, with cupboards and dressing
space as part of the room.

As it was quite a small room, it was simply
furnished to avoid clutter. The expanse of
window, the built-in cupboards and the
two doors reduced the opportunities for
furniture to a minimum. A double bed,
dressing table, bedside tables, chair and a
sheet of mirror running between study door
and cupboards constituted the rest of the
furniture. Character was created by the rich
grain of the wood, the bold stripe on the bed,
the bearskin rug, the vivid velvet headboard,
the lilac wall and the asymmetrically placed
baroque kneeling angel. The door alongside
this led into an en-suite bathroom, with a
floor of black-and-white thermoplastic tiles
that worked with the underfloor heating.

Below
The children's playroom opens on to the sun deck, which borders on to the kitchen, allowing outdoor play to be easily supervised. The patterned 'Numdah' rug on the playroom floor is from the Army & Navy Stores while all the toys are from Hamleys.

Bottom
This boy's room has a bed from Heal's and the walls are painted 'Lemon Peel', though it is impossible to tell this from the photograph. The 'Dog Basket' chair and toy cupboard are from Conran. An extra chair is stored on the wall, freeing up more floor space.

Children's rooms

In this house, the children's rooms combined the bare necessities with fantasy and fun. These rooms were only 2.7m (8ft 10in) square, with a run of cupboards on the unseen walls opposite the windows. Although they were small, they avoided being box-like with floor-to-ceiling windows, low beds and a minimum amount of furniture. The walls were matchboarded on two sides, and painted 'Cerulean Blue' in the girl's room, 'Lemon Peel' in the boy's. The blackboard wall in the boy's room looked decorative as well as giving him the freedom to sketch out ideas. His older sister's room was a little more grown up and housed books, marionettes, an old davenport and a collection of model horses. The walls were hung with her own paintings and birthday drawings done by friends. The playroom – which could double as a spare room when needed – linked the children's bedrooms and bathroom. At the back of the playroom, embracing ample cupboard space for toys, brooms, vacuum cleaner and so on, was the laundry, which was equipped with workbench and sink, washing machine and tumble dryer.

This house could be adapted to suit a family's different needs; whether they had older children, or perhaps an elderly parent who lived with them. The house's framed structure made these variations possible. As it was this framework alone that carried the first floor and the roof, the walls and windows within and without could be arranged in numerous ways without really altering the main character and form of the house. The system of underfloor heating assisted this flexibility; it could be divided into lots of different rooms or left as an open-plan space.

'A THOROUGHLY MODERN TERRACE'

'HOUSE OF IDEAS' | 1957

While the 1956 house was best suited for a rural or semi-suburban site, the second 'House of Ideas' was a prototype for modern urban housing. The first house was of timber, and had yet to be built, whereas the 1957 house was part of a new development at Blackheath, London, and could be bought. It was a modern brick terrace house and, although it occupied a tiny site, it made the most of it. The interior and exterior spaces were designed to work harmoniously together.

Above
The three-storey terrace house that formed the 1957 'House of Ideas' was a prototype for the Priory Estate, a new development in south-east London designed by Eric Lyons. The house's exterior situation, and outdoor planting, was as carefully considered as its interior.

Right
A view of the dining area showing the staircase and the built-in section of storage, which incorporates a serving hatch. The curved staircase eliminates the need for an entrance hall and was often used in modern buildings where space was limited. The walls are papered in 'Bamboo', a dull gold that was one of the *House & Garden* colours for 1957.

Left
An Edward Bawden mural decorates one end of the dining room. The room opens on to a patio in the centre of the house, which has the effect of bringing light into each room from multiple angles.

Below
A sun balcony opens off the main bedroom (*below left*), with a slatted wooden canopy and glass screen to shelter it from the wind (*bottom left*). Wall-mounted geraniums flower in the enclosed patio (*below right*), which can be seen from the sitting room (*bottom right*).

The architects saw it as more than just a house with some garden attached – it was a single unit, where house and garden were integrated. Great consideration was given to the exterior surroundings in this development. The front garden, patio and back garden were essentially open-air rooms with plants as carefully chosen and placed as the furniture indoors. They were selected for foliage rather than flowering value, to give the house some year-round privacy. The garden, therefore, was planted with a backbone of trees and shrubs, with small areas left for bedding and herbaceous plants, and the side and back walls for climbers. The use of paving in both front and back garden was a distinct part of the overall scheme, giving continuity to the whole site, and, with screen walls and planting in the front garden, it clearly defined the front and kitchen entrances.

The house echoed a traditional form of English building – the terrace house with mews at the back and accessible from the garden. Unlike its Georgian and Victorian predecessors, there was no basement for kitchen quarters and no upstairs drawing room. The kitchen and sitting rooms were on the ground floor, which extended as a single-storey wing into the back garden. A small glass-walled patio, which acted as the focus of the whole sitting area, admitted light and air into the centre of the house. The first-floor bedroom suite opened out on to the roof of this extension, which formed a sheltered sun terrace. On the top floor were two more bedrooms, and each bedroom floor had its own bathroom (one above the other and over the downstairs cloakroom to simplify plumbing and insulate noise).

Below
Two different trellis-patterned wallpapers create continuity in the decoration of the main bedroom (*below left* and *below right*) and the spare room (*below centre*). In the spare room is a Crown design incorporating a floral pattern, and to tie in with the spare room, the main bedroom has a hand-printed trellis wallpaper from Sanderson. This

room has an en-suite bathroom and is on the first floor, while the tiny spare room is on the floor above.

This house had both central and underfloor heating, and was designed to make the most of natural light. The sitting room and study opened on to the paved back garden. Above, screened by glass and roofed by a pergola, a balcony led off the main bedroom, while the patio created a brilliant pool of colour and light in the centre of the ground floor. Like its predecessor, the 1957 house was adaptable and could be laid out in different ways to suit a family's individual needs. As well as decorating the Blackheath house, *House & Garden* replicated the interiors at an exhibition in the Tea Centre on London's Regent Street. At Blackheath much of the furniture duplicated that at the Tea Centre exhibition, but colours and wall finishes used emphasized the architectural and structural details. The removal of the partition wall that separated the staircase and dining area from the main living space

also helped to bring out the full sculptural quality of the staircase and increased the open-plan effect. Strong colour was used on the ceiling and the long wall; colour again emphasized the structural beams and strong pattern of the fenestration and window joinery. The result was a space of interesting proportions and detail with a distinctive structural character that was partly based on the simplicity of Japanese architecture. In spite of this, it was a very English house. The designers also considered the particular character of Blackheath and its close association with Greenwich and the Thames, and tried to retain something of an early 19th-century feel in the approaches to the house.

Inside, the main living space had a floor of muhuhu, a light-coloured wood with lots of variation and life to it. This, with the timber staircase and brick wall linking the patio

Below left
The small bathroom on the second floor is enlivened with bright patterned curtains and a mustard ceiling.

Below centre
A simple white bedframe adds a modern elegance to the spare room.

Below right
The boy's bedroom on the second floor is decorated with two bird drawings by Michael Rothenstein and a handmade rug by Peter Collingwood.

with dining area and study, provided the key for all the furniture and decoration of the house. The soft, accommodating colours and patterns that formed much of the room schemes owed their origin to the natural colours of the timber. Wherever possible, British furniture was used. Two of the most interesting pieces were in the direct tradition of English chair making - the rush-bottomed chair designed by Dick Russell and the rocking chair by Edward Gardiner. The few Danish pieces used were very much in line with furniture produced by high-end British companies. The house also contained some works by British artists: the most important being a magnificent mural by Edward Bawden, which could be reproduced and assembled in sections; a hooked rug by Lucie Aldrighe; a small bronze by Daphne Hardy Henrion; prints by Michael Rothenstein; and paintings by

Mary Fedden, David Gentleman, Ian Baker and Michael Wickham.

The Blackheath house was designed for an imaginary client – a retired Royal Navy commander working at Greenwich, aged about 40, married, with a son of ten. Initially, these fictitious clients might have been a bit unsure about the open plan of the house, but they would have soon come to appreciate the extra space it afforded. He, with his naval background, would have recognized the economy of the neatly designed timber staircase, the compactness of the wardrobe fitting designed by the architect, and the shipshape way the television was housed. Everything in the house reflected this family's background and the way they lived, but it could have equally have formed a basic structure for a completely different family and tailored to suit different tastes.

Below
The space-saving kitchen is kitted out with the latest appliances, including a Falco cooker, Prescold refrigerator, English Electric washing machine and a Parnall 'Auto-Dry' tumble dryer. Although the walls are painted white, the ceiling is a bold 'Cornflower Blue'.

Right
A different angle of the sitting room, this time overlooking the garden. The room also doubled as a music area: a harpsichord stands in one corner, while cane chairs from Heal's invite people to sit and listen. A painting by Mary Fedden hangs above the sofa.

Left
The sitting area is a multipurpose space that combined a dining room, sitting room and study grouped around the patio. Sliding doors could cut off the study from the rest of the room. Maritime souvenirs decorate the shelves, including an antique map and various Nelson memorabilia.

Below
This view of the sitting room shows the floor-to-ceiling shelving units that occupy one corner of the room, as well as the muhuhu hardwood block flooring that provides a multi-tonal and hard-wearing surface. The walls are covered in white 'Leatherette' wallcovering from Sanderson.

'LIVING IN A SMALL SPACE'

CASE STUDY | FEBRUARY 1951

This basement flat belonged to designer Roger Nicholson and his wife Jane. At the time, Roger and his brother Robert were well known for their involvement with the upcoming Festival of Britain – they had designed a number of the room sets in the Homes and Gardens Pavilion.

Left
Beneath this John Nash terrace is a thoroughly modern flat.

Above
Roger Nicholson, who did much of the conversion work himself, works in an alcove in the sitting room, sketching designs for the upcoming Festival of Britain.

Right
The sitting room had asbestos walls, which were painted dark blue and pale blue, while the end of the working alcove was a rich red. The storage wall was designed by Roger Nicholson and had movable shelves of wood and glass.

Below
In the sitting room are two tables, end to end, made from shutters that were covered in hardboard and enamelled a sunny yellow. The grooved floor is made from pieces of hardboard. The shelving unit was designed by Roger, while some of his fabric designs hang on the wall, to the left of the window.

Right
The sink and cooker are linked up by grey linoleum-covered work surfaces; below these, curtains hide storage areas. Flower prints along the wall are protected by plate glass. Upper shelves have sliding metal doors.

Far right
The small kitchen, measuring only 2.7m (8ft 10in) long and 3m (9ft 10in) wide, is lined with pine matchboarding. A light encased in frosted glass (not seen) casts a diffused glow. The toughened-glass dining table folds against the wall; above it hangs a Perspex magazine rack.

In addition to his design work, Roger Nicholson was an artist who painted landscapes, portraits and abstracts, as well as designing textiles. He taught illustration at St Martin's School of Art (now Central Saint Martins), while his wife Jane was a designer in her own right. She was known for her embroidery and had written several books on the subject, in addition to designing textiles. With the Festival of Britain on everybody's minds, this feature was timed to make the most of public interest surrounding the event.

Despite providing guidance for a new era of interior design during the festival, Roger's own home was a little more modest. Still a young man, he had transformed

a poky, damp, ruined basement into a contemporary flat for himself, Jane and their two-year-old son. With the help of Jane and his brother Robert, he did everything himself, except the electrical fittings. He designed most of the furniture and succeeded in combating the damp by lining the walls with asbestos – still widely used as a building material during the Fifties – and covered the rotten, uneven floor with hardboard tiles.

Nicholson's ingenuity in using space made each room seem much larger than it really was, especially in the tiny kitchen. Each object was carefully chosen – as space was at a premium, every piece had to be both useful and decorative. Bookcases

were made ingenuously from glass and old ladders, which increased the impression of airiness. Large drawers were set into the old, blocked-up fireplace and a shelf set above it, while beside this was another unusual storage solution in the shape of a narrow vertical nook that held surprisingly ornamental filing boxes. A daring use of colour – a bright sunny yellow, rich red and blues – contributed to the spacious look that was so unusual in a basement.

'NEW TO OLD'

CASE STUDY | MARCH 1951

Ashley Havinden was one of the most successful advertising artists and designers in Britain during the Fifties. In 1951, he moved from his ultra-modern flat in Highgate, London, to Roxford – a Queen Anne country house in Hertfordshire – taking his modern furniture with him.

Left
At Roxford, a bright-red wall enlivens the entrance hall and stairs, giving a fresh look to the existing antique furniture; it is dominated by a huge John Piper painting. Beyond the hall lies the long sitting room, substantially updated by its new owner.

Above
Ashley Havinden, pictured here in the sitting room at Roxford, adapted his Queen Anne home to his modern tastes. Additions included the bookshelves shown here, which Havinden built himself.

Below
The owner transferred one of his most
treasured possessions, an Alexander
Calder mobile, from his previous,
ultra-modern flat in Highpoint, Highgate
(*bottom left* and *bottom right*), where it
hung in the sitting room, to Roxford.
Here it hangs in the stairwell.

Ashley Havinden was very forward thinking, as art director of Crawford's, a progressive advertising agency in London, he had created many innovative and stylish campaigns for companies such as Chrysler Motors, Martini and Pretty Polly – *House & Garden* called him 'twenty years ahead of his time' – and his house in Hertfordshire reflects this.

His move from modern to traditional resulted in an interior full of surprises. This was largely due to Havinden's impressive collection of modern art, which included paintings by Picasso, John Piper, Henry Moore, Ben Nicholson and Alexander Calder. This resolutely modern collection fitted surprisingly well in the rural, period setting of Roxford; mainly because Havinden had repainted the house in a deliberately fresh colour palette of pillar-box red, light blue and white. The house combined abstract art with 18th-century architectural features as well as incorporating all of the conveniences of Fifties living. What is interesting is how harmoniously the modern additions blended with the period pieces. Ancient double-sized floorboards, bookshelves made to Havinden's own design, exposed beams, Alexander Calder mobiles and an axe-hewn 16th-century refectory table sat side by side with the Duncan Miller armchairs designed in the Thirties. The eclectic contents of the house had been brought together by someone completely immersed in modern design, comfortable with using colour and who clearly understood the close relationship between textiles, paintings, posters, typography and architecture.

Below
In the sitting room, a radiogram, which
doubles as a side table, stands beside the
sofa. Above it, is a large painting by Ben
Nicholson; the rug on the floor, with its
abstract motif, was designed by Havinden
to complement it.

'SUNLIGHT AND AIR'

CASE STUDY | NOVEMBER 1951

Le Corbusier revolutionized 20th-century architecture. As well as being a prolific designer, he wrote widely on architecture and urban planning and lent his name to an entire style. His designs can be found throughout the world, from England to India, and the functional, tubular-steel furniture that he designed with Charlotte Perriand epitomizes the International Style.

Above
The entrance hall of Le Corbusier's Paris flat opens on to the spare room and a roof garden. Its simple, curving staircase is made of cast concrete and has no banister.

Right
Le Corbusier's studio on the eighth floor runs the whole width of the flat. The exterior wall is made of glass, with an opaque panel in the centre to break up the light. The painting is by Le Corbusier.

Below left
The end walls in the sitting room are of rough stone, and contrast with the expanse of the exterior glass wall. The painting and the sculpture are by Le Corbusier.

Below right
A view of the secluded sitting area and the sliding hall door, the sculpture is by the Cubist sculptor Jacques Lipchitz.

The Swiss-born Le Corbusier – real name Charles-Edouard Jeanneret-Gris – acknowledged a debt to the principles of volume and proportion used by the great 16th-century architect Palladio. Le Corbusier's flat in Paris, at Porte d'Auteuil, was at the top of a block he built himself. It was not only his home but also his laboratory and his guinea pig, for he believed that no building should be made for perpetual

generations of tenants. Although this flat was built in 1933, and the decoration had changed little in the 18 years that had elapsed since then, Le Corbusier's design and aesthetic was so ahead of his time that the flat was still considered extremely avant-garde in the Fifties. This was largely to do with Le Corbusier's choice of modern art and his taste for simple furniture, chosen for its fitness for purpose.

As his flat doubled as his workspace, it was very generously proportioned and partly open plan. The interior was characterized by a slightly transitory quality, as Le Corbusier chose objects not for permanence but because they happened to be of interest to him at that particular time. Because of the functional nature of the apartment, Le Corbusier would only have decorative items of immediate interest present, and these

Below left
Soft cowhides divide the floor of the sitting area from the rest of the open-plan room. Le Corbusier, in collaboration with Charlotte Perriand, designed the large armchair in 1929. The bentwood dining chairs are by Thonet.

Below right
In a corner of a bedroom, an asymmetrical door, which adds to the modern, open-plan feel of the room, leads into an en-suite bathroom, with walls tiled in mosaic.

Bottom right
In the bedroom, a painting by Fernand Léger hangs on the back of a cupboard. It was given to the Le Corbusiers as a wedding present.

were replaced when they no longer held any significance for the designer.

The open-plan configuration encompassed a studio, living area and dining space. There was one huge living room in which he also dined, and which had, for winter evenings, a comfortable alcove away from the outside glass walls. Cowhides were used to denote the sitting area, which was furnished with the large armchairs that Le Corbusier and Charlotte Perriand had designed in 1929. The bentwood dining chairs were by Thonet. The large abstract paintings seen on the easel and on the rough-stone end walls were by Le Corbusier; other art in the apartment included a piece by the Cubist sculptor Jacques Lipchitz and a painting by Fernand Léger, given as a wedding present.

Throughout the flat there was the feeling of the interplay of volumes, and the whole flat bore out, in miniature, Le Corbusier's belief that all people have a right to space, sunshine and air.

'DESIGNERS AT HOME'

CASE STUDY | JANUARY 1954

This four-storey house overlooking the Thames belonged to two of the most famous designers of the Fifties, Robin and Lucienne Day. This house in Cheyne Walk displays the Days' shared vision and presents a unique opportunity to see how the ultimate interiors power couple of the Fifties chose to decorate their own home.

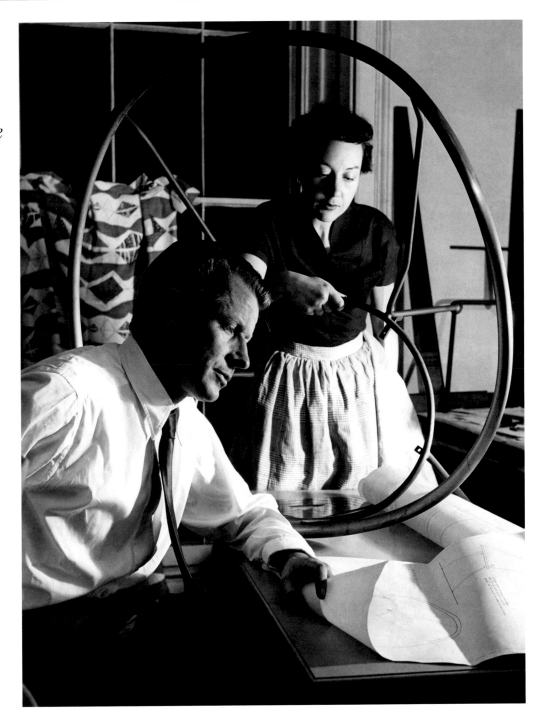

Left
Although the Days' Chelsea home dated from 1862, they reconfigured it to allow for an open-plan living area; seen here is the dining end of the living room, where white cords stretched across black paint create the effect of a false ceiling.

Right
Lucienne examines a sketch for a new furniture design by her husband, Robin. Pieces of Robin's furniture can be seen in their studio and behind the couple hangs a patterned fabric of Lucienne's design.

Below
The entrance hall leads to the ground-floor studio, while stairs lead up to the living area. The banisters are painted black, white and lemon yellow (*left*). A cupboard and shelf unit in the living room (*right*).

Centre
The Victorian exterior of the four-storey house (*left*). The fireplace wall of the living room; the moulded-metal chair covered in tweed was designed by Charles Eames (*right*).

Bottom
In the kitchen, a dumbwaiter brings food down to the next floor; it is screened with a panel, papered in a Steinberg photomural (*left*). The bedroom opens out to a passage that leads to the kitchen; you can see Robin Day standing behind the corrugated Perspex room divider in the kitchen (*right*).

Robin Day was a celebrated furniture designer whose work for British furniture company Hille transformed the company into a pioneer of modern furniture. Lucienne Day was the leading British textile designer of the decade, designing around six fabrics for Heal's each year, as well as patterns for wallpapers, ceramics and carpets.

The ground floor of their Cheyne Walk house served as their studio, while the first-floor rooms were made into one large living area with windows at either end. This room had white walls to show off the lines of the simple furniture and the few bright colours in the cushions and curtains. A false ceiling of stretched white cords in the dining area created a dramatic effect below a black-painted ceiling, set off by curtains in flame-coloured percale. A short wall was covered with woven reeds that disguised the dumbwaiter – the lift that brought food down from the kitchen on the second floor. All furniture in the dining area was designed by Robin Day and made by Hille. In the living area, the ceiling was full height and painted white; curtains were of grey-and-white linen, maps of the Thames at Chelsea covered the back of the sideboard, and on the floor was a black-and-white-striped rug by Mourne Textiles. All the furniture was modern, comprising a Thonet chair, a settee in grey tweed and a reclining chair in green and black – the latter were both from Hille. Near the windows stood three pebble-filled troughs for plants and to the left, against a grey-painted wall, was a metal unit fitted with cupboards and lots of shelves for books. The understated confidence of this interior showed the sophistication and seamless collaboration between two design legends.

Below
The sitting area of the open-plan first
floor looks out towards the river; the floor
is made of large blocks of tiled wood.

'A NEW LEASE'

CASE STUDY | SEPTEMBER 1954

This article appeared just a year before Hans Knoll died in a car crash at the age of 41, and showed an apartment belonging to a couple who were at the height of their creative careers. Hans and Florence Knoll had together founded Knoll Associates, a New York design and furnishing firm that manufactured the work of the most celebrated 20th-century designers, including Eero Saarinen, Mies van der Rohe and Harry Bertoia.

Right
Round the waxed walnut table are upholstered dining chairs by Eero Saarinen, covered in granite-coloured tweed. They are a similar design to the armchair shown in the picture opposite. Above the sideboard is a 17th-century Spanish painting.

Far right
In the open-plan living area of this Paris apartment, much of the furniture is of a forward-looking, modern design. The small armchair by the table was designed by Eero Saarinen. Plants and flowers are used to soften the severely simple lines of the furniture.

Below
Refreshingly simple in colour and form, this fitted banquette occupies a corner of the living area, with cushions in a variety of colours. Patterned sisal matting covers most of the floor.

Below right
Chairs with cow-hide seats fastened over their tubular-metal frames stand in front of a fishnet curtain dividing part of one end of the living room from the other.

Bottom left
In Hans and Florence Knoll's bedroom, a large, accommodating armchair, by Saarinen, forms a chaise longue when used with its matching stool. The room is lit mainly by the Anglepoise lamp; the baroque iron wall bracket serves purely as an ornament.

Bottom right
Surprisingly modern in design, this 17th-century Italian candelabra is suspended, by an invisible nylon thread, in order to light the table for meals.

Although the Knolls were based in the States, they also owned this flat in Paris. The flat was formerly the attic of a 17th-century house in St-Germain-des-Prés and it was previously occupied by an artist. Once the Knolls had acquired their Parisian artist's garret, they were faced with the problem of converting the large open studio into smaller, cosier areas.

In true modern style, they were keen to retain something of an open-plan effect, even though they wanted to create some divisions for privacy. They achieved this by suspending a fishnet curtain from the buttress of the ceiling between two skylight windows, thus giving the impression of two separate areas without entirely breaking the continuity of space. Furniture included dining chairs and armchairs by Eero Saarinen, while patterned sisal matting on the floors added to the modern feel. An abundance of plants and cut flowers brought life and energy to the space, and the couple retained some touches of the flat's history. They decided to leave the dado rail in place – it was commonly considered outdated and therefore removed in many

Fifties conversions – though they painted it the same colour as the wall to make it less obvious. Another nod to the building's 17th-century provenance was found in a religious painting from the same period, which hung above the modern sideboard. In this flat, comfort was as much of a priority as style, and this can be seen in the upholstered chairs and the Anglepoise lamps that provided focused lighting where needed. Although the floor space was limited, there were still many places for the couple to sit, relax and entertain.

'SMALL HOUSE IN HAMPSTEAD'

CASE STUDY | NOVEMBER 1955

On a sloping site in Hampstead that was once part of a kitchen garden was a small house designed by the modern architect Alexander Gibson. It was surrounded by tall trees – unusual for a London house – and stood out amid the Georgian and Victorian buildings to either side of it.

Left
At one end of the open-plan living and dining area, white shelves stand out against the background wall, painted a dark grey. Large French windows open out on to the back garden.

Right
The kitchen is visually separated from the dining room by a storage unit, which also doubles as a food preparation area (*above*). The tiny raised entrance hall, seen from the living room, has a brick wall and polished slate floor (*below*).

Below
To the left, a brightly coloured Lurçat tapestry hangs on a pale-lilac wall; before it is a marble-topped Empire side table. The egg-shaped dining table and 'Ant' chairs are Danish, while the curtains are a design by Eileen Bell for Whitehead.

Bottom left
This shelved opening connects the living area with the kitchen and displays a collection of pots and bowls. A pale-blue Vernini oil lamp is displayed on the antique shaving stand.

Bottom right
A view of the sitting room from the raised hallway; the glazed floor-to-ceiling windows allow plenty of natural light to flood into the L-shaped sitting and dining area, which is located to the right of this picture.

Although the design of this house was very modern, it was carefully planned so that it would fit in with its neighbours. Sadly, it was demolished in 2008, so nothing remains of this triumph of modern design. The compact house was built for a married couple with no children and had only two bedrooms. The ground floor was open plan, with kitchen merging into dining room, which in turn merged into the sitting room, making the whole space seem enormous. As the owners were keen gardeners, they had, in addition to their garden, a large open roof terrace-cum-patio where climbing plants and shrubs could be seen from both bedrooms.

Just as the house itself was cleverly planned to sit easily alongside the older buildings around it, so its interior was a harmonious background for both antique and modern furniture. Eileen Bell decorated the house and furnished it from Woollands of Knightsbridge – an Edwardian department store that had recently been revamped as a fashionable destination showcasing the work of upcoming designers. Eileen Bell was an artist as well as an occasional interior designer, and for this project she chose a restrained palette, mainly pale subdued colours and white, to set off the dark antiques, rich glass, vibrant Lurçat tapestry, ormolu and zebrano wood. There is little pattern except for Bell's own textile designs, which add life and detail to the rooms. This house was designed to be very energy efficient; it was cleverly insulated and the floor-to-ceiling windows were also double-glazed, meaning that heating bills for this modern house would have been a fraction of those of its rather more stately next-door neighbours.

Below
On the first floor is an L-shaped roof garden that is accessible from both the main bedroom and the spare room. The sculpture is by Ruth Windmiller Duckworth.

Bottom left
From the back garden, the modern lines of the house are softened by the way in which the new building has been integrated with the existing planting; the mature trees were preserved, as was part of the old kitchen-garden wall.

Bottom right
The house was built in red brick in order to blend in with the façades of the Georgian and Victorian houses that stand to either side of it.

'THE BRIGHTER LOOK'

CASE STUDY | MARCH 1956

This Holland Park town house belonged to the Boissevain family, and during the Fifties it stood out among the cream and buff stucco fronts of its neighbours due to the colourful treatments of its late Regency façade.

Above right
Colours from the *House & Garden* range decorate Antoinette Boissevain's ground-floor bedsit. Colours used include 'Gunmetal', 'Leaf', 'Flame', 'Lemon Peel' and 'Citron'.

Right
In the dining room, 'Terracotta' and 'Mustard' – two more *House & Garden* shades – provide the background for dark antique furniture. On the right is the storage wall that partitions off the kitchen.

Far right
A portrait group of Antoinette Boissevain's great-grandfather's family is the focal point of her room and inspired the colour palette. Inherited furniture sits alongside contemporary pieces designed by her son John.

Below left
The staircase is treated with extreme simplicity, relying for effect on the juxtaposition of plain areas of colour – 'Citron', 'Guardsman', 'Cornflower' and white, with a carpet in 'Terracotta'.

Below right
This attic room belonged to Daniël and Antoinette's youngest son, John, who was an architect. As his room also doubles as a study for drawing plans, he chose to rein in his taste for bright colours in favour of predominantly white walls, to reflect the limited amount of natural light afforded by the small window.

Bottom
John's brother Roland chose a restrained, though essentially modern, scheme for his room, using mainly natural textures and white, with one wall covered in a lime-coloured, patterned paper.

Below
This alternate view of John's room shows how he used small quantities of intense colour to create a modern effect. This approach works well with the shape of the room; its sloping ceilings, eaves and L-shape create many irregular surfaces.

Bottom
At the back of the house is a small garden, with a raised balcony area that opens off from Antoinette's ground-floor rooms. This was used for outdoor dining, weather permitting.

Both the exterior and interior paint was from the *House & Garden* range; the interior had also undergone a colourful overhaul so that the personality of each member of the family was reflected in his or her own room. This house had been completely refurbished after being requisitioned during the Second World War; the family had not been able to move back in until 1955, when they were faced with ruined interiors and a bad case of dry rot. The house had to be completely redecorated, but given the Boissevains' provenance in design, they were well equipped to do so.

Daniël and Antoinette Boissevain were both Dutch immigrants who had formed a lighting company, Merchant Adventurers, in 1929. By the Fifties, it had become well established. They had four sons: Walter and Roland worked for the family company and Paul and John had become architects – with Paul also designing lights for Merchant Adventurers. It was John, the youngest, who had modernized the family home and had designed all the furniture units, which blend with the existing antiques. As the two younger sons had grown up but still lived at home, and Daniël and Antoinette both needed spaces to work, the house is set out as a series of individual bedsits. The basement, formerly the kitchen, was turned into a flat for the caretakers, while a kitchen was made on the ground floor and sectioned off at one side of the dining room behind a colourful storage wall. This enabled easier food preparation while still preserving a dedicated space for meals, which was often the only time the family would sit together before returning to their own pursuits. Mrs Boissevain's room was also on the ground floor and opened on to a balcony, which was occasionally used as an outdoor dining area in summer.

On the first floor was Mr Boissevain's room, which doubled as an office, and also a communal sitting room for formal entertaining and a bathroom. Roland Boissevain's room, the housekeeper's room and another bathroom lay on the second floor, while John Boissevain occupied the low-ceilinged penthouse at the top. This unusual layout enabled the occupants to live independent lives while still functioning as a family unit – a thoroughly radical way to restore a traditional town house.

'IT BEGAN WITH TWO MUD HUTS'

CASE STUDY | DECEMBER 1956

The black-and-white photographs by Charles Eames, featured here, mask the bright colours of this house at Santa Fe, New Mexico, which was designed and decorated by its owner, the architect Alexander Girard.

Left
A view of the sitting room, which opens on to the entrance hall, with a staircase leading to the first-floor studio.

Above right
The dining patio seen from the kitchen end; to the foreground is a chair by Charles Eames, who took the photographs for this feature.

Right
The view from the house encompasses the pink hills of Santa Fe, scattered with dwarf pines, cacti and wild flowers growing between the rocky outcrops.

Below
In the sitting room, a storage wall displays a bright collection of toys, paintings and other small objects.

Bottom
A day bed and a George Nelson lamp furnish the sitting room; beyond is the colourfully decorated dining room.

No one is entirely sure why Charles Eames had turned his hand to interiors photography – however, it was likely that he was staying with Girard while he and his wife Ray were making some short films of Mexico, among them the documentary *The Day of the Dead* (1957), for which Girard was the producer. The intricate, handmade models in this film are reflected in the many dolls that Girard – also a talented textile designer – made specifically to decorate this house. After his death, these wooden dolls, never intended for commercial production, were placed in the Vitra Design Museum and have since been put into production by Vitra.

Eames's stay at Girard's Santa Fe house had an even more significant impact on the development of Fifties design in the United States. Although Girard had trained as an architect, he is now best known for his textile designs for Herman Miller. Girard's bold use of colour and playful motifs – inspired by the folk art of Mexico and India – added a clever juxtaposition with the starkly modern furniture that displayed it. It was Eames who brought Girard to Herman Miller – shortly after he had taken these pictures of the Santa Fe house.

This unusual house incorporated two older buildings, both built with traditional adobe walls of sun-dried mud bricks. The new additions created a central patio, with further covered spaces to enable comfortable outdoor sitting and dining in any weather. The indigenous character of the house was retained in the rough timber, local stone and painted mud walls, which blended easily with the new structure, reinterpreting a traditional style of building in a very modern way. Inside, a large lamp

Below left
The loggia, with a multicoloured and patterned wall – the house's rustic design is a result of the extensive use of locally sourced materials.

Below right
In the sitting room, a masonry table also doubles as a back rest for a floor seat; the informal layout of this house encouraged flexible seating arrangements.

Bottom
A view of the dining room, with the sitting room beyond. The chairs are by Charles Eames; the table is suspended on nylon-coated cable.

by George Nelson forms a focal point at the intersection between the sitting room and dining room. Other modern touches include the dining-room table, suspended on nylon-coated cable and surrounded by a set of Eames chairs.

As Girard's signature style was a colourful amalgamation of folk art and modern design, it seems apt that his own home was the most complete expression of how two seemingly different aesthetics could easily coexist in a symbiotic relationship that looked both natural and visually compelling.

'SETTING UP HOUSE THE HARD WAY'

CASE STUDY | JUNE 1957

Terence Conran is one of the most influential 20th-century designers, with a career spanning six decades. He founded Habitat and The Conran Shop, and has written over 50 books on design. In this article, Terence and Shirley Conran describe how they set up their first home.

Above
Terence and Shirley Conran with their son Sebastian in 1957 (*left*). An open-plan living room incorporates a dining area; while a metal and African walnut shelving unit creates a division between this and the kitchen. On the shelves are Victorian grocers' tins and chemists' jars, used for storage (*right*)

Right
A view of the open-plan dining area and kitchen. A Nigerian blanket is used as a rug on the birch-plywood floor, the dining chairs are by Giò Ponti and the large spherical hanging lamp is by Noguchi. The wall behind the white kitchen units is faced with ceramic tiles in *House & Garden*'s 'Deep Night', from the magazine's colour range.

Left
A painting by Martin Bradley hangs on the studio wall; under it on the polished pine floor is an 18th-century chest and a 'Tripolina' canvas chair.

Below left
Flemish pottery, Victorian mugs and Roman and Georgian glass form an interesting collection on a shelf unit in the living room, alongside a Thonet rocking chair found in a junk shop.

Below right
In the grey-carpeted bedroom, the curtains in seven shades of green and blue were designed by Astrid Sampe. A Canadian blanket is used as a bedspread.

Bottom
On the floor of the top-floor sitting room lies a kilim rug, its warm tones contrasting with the rough white-painted brickwork and plaster surround of the fireplace. The tall basket for logs came from Madeira. Charles Eames designed the metal chair under the window.

'We are not just another young couple who stumbled across an 18th-century house dirt cheap and remodelled it with grit, initiative and £50. We didn't tear down dingy Victorian fireplaces to find – surprise – superb Adam mantelpieces sitting snugly behind them, and there was no attic in which to discover a dusty but exquisite Sheraton table that only needed stripping to look perfect. We never actually bid for anything at a country auction; the prices were always too high when the bidding started. And finally, we did not paint the whole house and re-lay the floor in one weekend, only taking time off to knock up picnic meals of Chicken à la King or cheese soufflé. It took all our spare time for nearly two months to lay the living room floor; our marriage nearly broke up before it started because of the many bitter words about the right way to apply Phenoglaze. But we admit to a predilection for junk shops, although most of the ones we first visited seemed to contain nothing but junk which was expensive at half the price.

'We made four small rooms at the top of the house (part of a solidly built Regency terrace) into one large open-plan living room. We have discovered two disadvantages; our son Sebastian normally stays in his nursery, except at meals, but when we gave a party in the living room for his first birthday we had to barricade the staircase with the sofa to prevent the children falling down stairs. The second disadvantage is that, although in theory it is a good idea to be able to cook and listen to the conversation going on in the living room, in fact, the conversation tends to be distracting to the cook who is tempted to wander away from the stove and join in some

fascinating gossip only to be abruptly recalled by something burning or boiling over.

'Open-plan living has proved most successful with us, but this is partly because we have plenty of room in the rest of the house, even though the basement is occupied by our housekeeper and the ground floor is let as a self-contained flat. Our bedroom is on the second floor and we work in the first-floor studio. However, the atmosphere of quiet concentration there may soon be shattered unless we install sound-proof doors, because the next room is the nursery.'

'ARTIST IN RESIDENCE'

CASE STUDY | OCTOBER 1958

English sculptor Reg Butler shot to international fame after winning a competition to design a monument to the Unknown Political Prisoner. Models of Butler's proposed sculpture were displayed at the Tate in 1953 and the 122m (400ft) steel monument was intended to be erected in West Berlin, although, ultimately, it was never built.

Left
Butler leans through the hatch that separates his studio – built in the kitchen wing of an old manor house – from the new extension to the house, which accommodates an open-plan sitting area.

Above right
The generous size and height of the studio enable the sculptor to work on his larger-than-life-size figures, including this female form.

Right
A Marcel Breuer chaise longue in the living room. A shelf runs the length of the sitting-room wall, housing a collection of succulents and cacti.

Following pages
A pair of upholstered tub chairs by Robin Day, along with the two Marcel Breuer chaise longues, add to the modern decoration in the sitting room. The framed pictures on the wall are all by Reg Butler.

Below
In the sun-catching courtyard, a canvas
awning shades the corner made by the old
and new buildings.

This much-lauded, proposed commission was a protracted process; when this article was published, more than five years after Butler had won the competition, plans were still underway to build his modernist vision. If it had gone ahead, it would have been one of the biggest pieces of sculpture in the world, but political controversy meant that it never materialized.

It was during this time that *House & Garden* visited Reg Butler's studio in Berkhamsted, Hertfordshire, where he lived with his family. Living quarters, garden and studio were all packed with evidence of his work; finished or half-finished pieces were everywhere. The Butlers occupied a wing of an old manor house, formerly the old kitchens, to which they had added an extension to house a sitting room.

This extension, along with an old wall that divided the kitchen garden from the formal garden beside it, formed a paved and grassed courtyard – which was dominated by a Butler's towering statue, *Girl Undressing*. The original, thick-walled kitchen was converted into the artist's studio. Outside the studio a new concrete terrace accommodated finished, or partly finished, sculptural figures. Also on the terrace were metal chairs, with slung canvas seats, which were designed and made by the sculptor.

Inside, the house was simply furnished in a functional, modern way. Butler's sculptures decorated the sitting room and the drawings on the walls were his, too. The floor was concrete, painted grey, and pipes for central heating were installed around the base of the walls. Two of Marcel Breuer's classic pre-war chaise longues, upholstered in blue, and Robin Day's yellow tub chairs from Hille, provided stylish seating. This was a house designed as a workspace as well as a family home, and combined functionality and modern design in a understated and completely unique way.

Below left
An assortment of industrial lights enables focused lighting to be used by the sculptor in the thick-walled studio.

Below right
A wall of windows lends an airy, conservatory atmosphere to the sitting-room extension.

Bottom left
To the left of the Robin Day chair is a wireless; ink drawings hang above the shelving unit behind it.

Bottom right
Maquettes for sculptures stand on a set of custom-built shelves in the sitting room.

'THE HOUSE WITH FOLDING WALLS'

CASE STUDY | APRIL 1959

By the Fifties, Giò Ponti was known as the pioneer of modern Italian design. His prolific output spanned many mediums – from furniture and architecture to ceramics and glass. Throughout this decade he also collaborated with another Italian designer, Piero Fornasetti, and together the two men brought Italian design – which had re-emerged after the destructive effects of the Second World War – to an international audience.

Above
This modern apartment in Italy was designed by Giò Ponti specifically to suit his family's needs; this view of the sitting area shows the large windows that flooded the apartment with light.

Left
Sliding partitions offer the option to divide the space into a series of rooms or else to create one large, open-plan living area.

Right
Most of the furniture in the apartment is of white elm, including a row of Ponti's iconic 'Superleggera' chairs.

Left
Modern art and eye-catching furniture, such as this three-drawer cabinet, enliven a corner of one of the bedrooms.

Right
A bedroom has a sliding partition, enabling the room to be separated or connected to the vast, open-plan living area. The headboard is built into the wall and concealed lighting prevents unnecessary clutter, adding to the room's streamlined effect.

Giò Ponti had already made his name before the start of the war – he had been the art director of the leading ceramics manufacturer Richard-Ginori from 1923 to 1930 – but the Fifties saw him at the height of his creative powers. He created his best-known design, the 'Superleggera' chair, in 1957. This simple lightweight chair, still in production today, is both classic and modern, and its minimal, yet elegant, lines encapsulate modern Italian design.

This design aesthetic can also be seen in Ponti's own apartment, which he built, furnished and decorated to his own plans. Nothing was brought from his previous home except objects that were of particular artistic interest or sentimental value. This apartment was home to five people: Ponti, his wife, their young daughter and son and a live-in housekeeper. Although it wasn't a particularly large space, it was divided up by movable partitions to create a series of flexible rooms, giving a sense of spaciousness and light. Three sliding partitions allowed the entire front area of the apartment, consisting of four rooms – the two children's bedrooms, the sitting room and his wife's bedroom – to be formed into a long unrestricted area. Signora Ponti's bedroom could be united with Ponti's own bedroom and studio to form one large

room and the studio could, in turn, be incorporated with the living room.

A ceramic floor of diagonally striped tiles ran throughout the entire apartment, visually uniting it, and the ceiling continued the diagonal line throughout with matt and gloss stripes in white plaster. The colours used throughout the apartment were white and different shades of yellow. The front façade of the apartment was a long, continuous window broken up by shelves on which ornaments were silhouetted against the sky. Shelves had built-in lighting that gave the impression that they were

detached from the wall and floating into the room. Even the headboards of the beds were built into the walls in this clever way and were equipped with concealed lighting arrangements and ornaments.

All furniture and wooden sections of the house were in white elm. The contrasting interest and shapes were supplied by the many pieces of carefully chosen ceramics, terracotta and straw ornaments, and paintings, as well as curios collected over the years from many parts of the world, resulting in an interior that combined Italian design with an international outlook.

'MODERN MASTERPIECE'

As the final touches were made to the new US Embassy in London, Eero Saarinen was celebrated for his innovative designs, as can be seen in this airy house in America's Midwest.

Right
A view of the house with, to the left, the dining loggia and, to the right, part of the huge open-plan living area (*top*). Showcasing the generous space and lateral configuration of this house, floor-to-ceiling windows in the living area – with its sunken central seating area – afford spectacular views of the surrounding countryside (*bottom*).

Far right
Wide sliding doors open to join the living room and loggia. From overhead, fine jets of water rain down into the pool, and the comfortable feeling of sheltered outdoor living is enhanced by the wide eaves with their inset skylights.

© EZRA STOLLER/ESTO

Previous pages
From the east wing you look across the pool into the huge, open-plan living area with sunken sitting area. A 15m (50ft) shelving unit makes the most of the impressive space, while, to the left, a Kashmir shawl affixed to a panel screens the main entrance from view. The clever positioning of skylights, combined with floor-to-ceiling windows, means that each room is light-filled and airy regardless of aspect. While all this glass lends the house an open-plan feel, it still manages to create a number of self-contained, private areas.

Below left
A curtain closes off the dining room from the living room when required. The circular dining table incorporates a floral centrepiece and fountain, where a brass pipe concealed in the table base pumps water to fountain jets in the table bowl on the table.

Below right
In the living area, the marble walls are silicone-treated and the floor made of travertine – both of these finishes were hard-wearing and easy to clean, a useful feature in a house of such large proportions.

Right
Brightly coloured table decorations and a colourful assortment of cutlery and tableware offset the neutral decoration of the dining room and living room beyond.

Eero Saarinen's work as an architect and designer helped shape what we now think of as the Fifties aesthetic. From collaborating with Charles Eames on a Case Study House in California to designing the US Embassy in London, his influence still resonates through modern design today. He had a long-running relationship with Knoll and many of his furniture designs are still in production.

Saarinen was born in Finland, went to the States with his parents when he was 13, studied sculpture in Paris and took a Fine Art degree at Yale University, then started his career with his father's architectural firm. He was soon much in demand as an architect, and his work included this uncompromisingly modern house in the Midwest. At the heart of this building was a vast central living room, shaped like a very irregular cross. Glass walls and loggias to the north, south and west added to the overwhelming sense of size and lightness of this open-plan space.

The essential plan of the house was divided into five parts, carefully adapted to the family's living arrangements. These smaller rooms are very self-contained. In the children's area, the bedrooms, bathrooms and storage area were wrapped around the playroom. The parents occupied a separate area, which had a sitting room, bedroom and a quiet study. Each of them had a large walk-in dressing room. The spare room occupied its own corner just a few steps from the south terrace.

Unsurprisingly, much of the furniture was designed by Saarinen and the base palette of the interior is neutral, with a few splashes of bright red or yellow to add a bit of life and vibrancy, without being overwhelming. The result is a house that was entirely of its time yet still looks fresh and contemporary today.

3. DECORATION

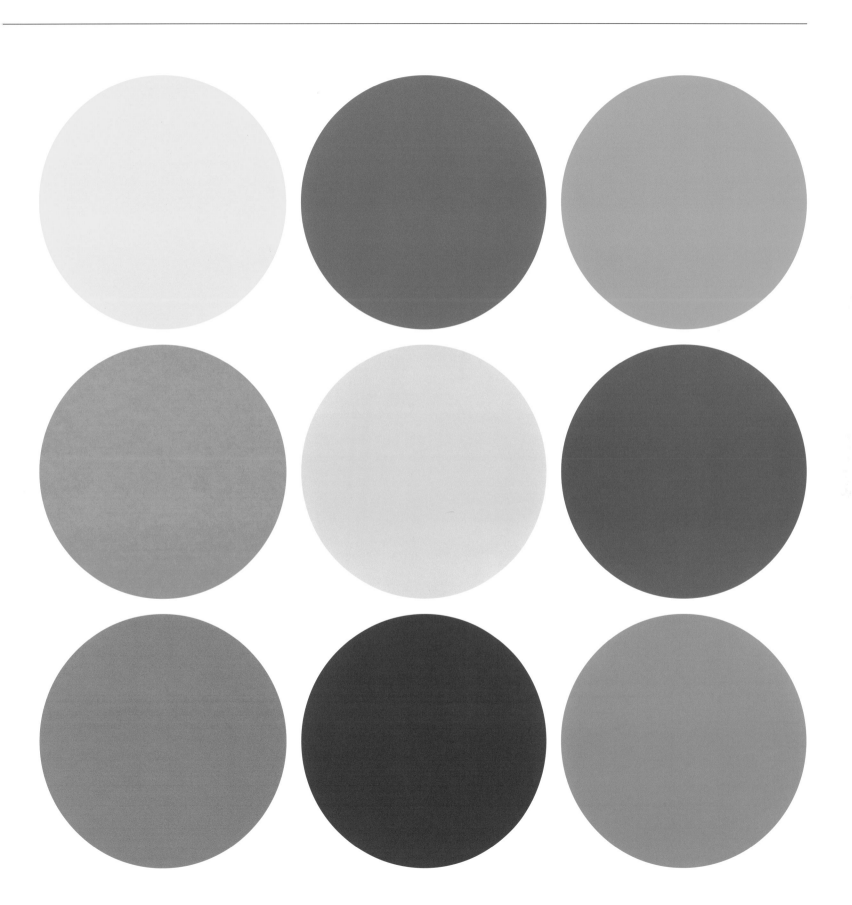

FURNITURE

In furniture design, the Fifties marked the high point of what is now referred to as Mid-century Modern. In Britain, Mid-century furniture evolved out of the Utility scheme that was in place from 1941 to 1951, as furniture was rationed in a similar way to other commodities, such as food.

Right
(1) 'Allegro' printed linen by Lucienne Day, (2) Carving table by Christopher Heal, (3) Desk lamp by John Reid, (4) Standard lamp by Bernard Schottlander, (5) 'Alvar' wallpaper by Barbara Hirsch, (6) 'Roebuck' dining chair by Ernest Race, (7) 'Cymbeline' textured fabric by Tibor Reich, (8) 'Pegasus' settee by Howard Keith, (9) Standard lamp by John Reid, (10) Plant stand by Terence Conran, (11) 'Stella' wallpaper by Lucienne Day, (12) 'Hillestack' dining chair by Robin Day, (13) 'Fall' printed cotton by Lucienne Day, (14) 'SP107' printed fabric by Jacqueline Groag.

Far right
A 'NK25' chair from Finmar, with ebonized legs, and a Robin Day for Hille tub chair stand next to a terrazzo-topped table by Slinga Furniture (which also designed the white-and-black table). A mustard Robin Day chair, a Conran Furniture metal-frame chair, a chair made by HK and a 'Grenville' settee, by David Pye for Christie Taylor, complete this very modern room.

Left
In 1955 a flexible shelving and seating
solution is provided by a cupboard,
three-drawer chest and benches, by
Robin Day for Hille, which were sold as a
set. The cupboards have mahogany cases
and ash or rosewood fronts. The settee
and chair are by Buoyant, while the
Warerite-topped table with a leaf design
has brass legs and is by Philip Pound. A

'Squatter' stool from HK is upholstered in
two colours of corduroy, chosen to match
the bright colours of the painted column
and mural.

Below
'Rhorkee' camp chair, from Army &
Navy Stores.

To understand British design in the Fifties, it is necessary to look at the wartime restrictions that were still in place at the start of the decade. Utility designs were limited to a very narrow range, made by approved manufacturers to a specific construction method. People who were deemed to be in need of new furniture – newlyweds, people whose houses had suffered bomb damage and so on – were issued with coupons and selected furniture from the approved Utility catalogue. The designs were simple, unadorned and robustly constructed – this necessary functionality created furniture that echoed the principles of modernism. Before the Second World War, modernism had not proved popular with the British public, who preferred reproduction furniture. A flick through a Utility catalogue would probably appal modernist aficionados – the designs were effectively a compromise of tastes, melding the straight clean lines of modernism with an upholstered squareness of design so beloved of the British public. In practice, the Utility scheme seemed to resemble a mechanized version of the Arts and Crafts movement, where fitness for purpose combined with rather rustic, dark-stained furniture that was very English. This desire to disguise any international influences seeping in was reflected in the names of the furniture collections – the first range of Utility furniture was called 'Chiltern' and the second 'Cotswold'.

'A ROLE FOR THE ELBOW CHAIR'

SEPTEMBER 1959

Right
(1) Teak 'K8027A', designed by Svend A Madsen, made by Heal's, (2) Oak 'K9921', made by Heal's, (3) Mahogany '6244', designed by Peter Hayward, made by Vanson, (4) Teak '56', designed by N O Moller, made by Danasco, (5) Teak 'FJ48', designed by Finn Juhl, made by Fin, (6) Teak 'Lansom', designed by John Herbert, made by A Younger, (7) Ebonized-wood 'Tigullina', designed by Chiavari, made by Conran, (8) Beech 'Langford' (with tapestry seat), made by Parker Knoll, (9) Mahogany 'Ablemarle', designed by Robin Day, made by Hille, (10) Sheraton-style yew chair, made by Titchmarsh & Goodwin, (11) Beech 'Link 7 Tola', made by Harris Lebu, (12) Smoked-oak and teak 'K9906', designed by Anton Borg and Arne Vodder, made by Heal's, (13) Teak 'Gazelle', designed by Rastad & Relling, made by Danasco, (14) Steel and wood 'Executive C14A', made by Conran, (15) Mahogany '1204', designed by Tom Lupton and John Morton, made by LM Furniture.

Below
Balancing on a Lambretta scooter, this model holds up a super-light 'IC8' dining chair by Giò Ponti as an example of modern Italian design in 1959. This was Ponti's iconic 'Superleggera' that was licensed to be manufactured by Conran Furniture. The woven baskets with the rope handles are from Liberty and Woollands. Opposite her is an 'Obelisk Concealed Lamp' by Fornasetti, set conveniently on casters for added mobility.

Right
A 1955 shopping feature on 'masters of modern design', showed pieces from seven different designers. *Clockwise from top left*, these are: Giò Ponti ('Superleggera' chair); Joseph Motte (cane chair); Astrid Sampe (fabric); Charles Eames (metal-frame chair); Ico Parisi (circular chair); Le Corbusier (wooden chair); and Arne Jacobsen ('Ant' chair).

Once these restrictions were lifted, an international influence revolutionized British furniture. Home-grown talents included Robin Day – whose designs for Hille made the company famous for its exciting new furniture in metal and plastic – and Ernest Race, whose metal 'Antelope' chair pointed the way for a new range of furniture that could be used either outdoors or indoors. Race produced popular designs throughout the Fifties – including the 'Springbok' and 'Heron' chairs – and was commissioned to furnish the British Pavilion in the World Fair in Brussels in 1958. Another British company, Gomme of High Wycombe, launched the G Plan range in 1953. Initially, it was made of oak but later output, influenced by the Scandinavian style, was often of teak. G Plan advertised widely, emphasizing the versatility and flexibility of its system, which allowed people to buy individual items as needed rather than complete suites. Ercol was also popular during this decade, although it was seen as more of a functional than fashionable brand. Still, its roots in Utility furniture – Ercol made the '4a Windsor' kitchen chair – meant that it was to be found in a large number of homes.

International furniture designers also left their mark on the British interior, and influenced British companies. In the States, Charles and Ray Eames were an important influence – designs produced during this decade included the 'Elliptical Table' and 'Wire Mesh Chair' in the early Fifties, the iconic '670 Lounge Chair' and '671 Ottoman' appeared in 1956 and the 'Aluminium Group' followed in 1958. Harry Bertoia worked for the Eameses as a young man and

Left
The storage unit from Remploy was originally produced for factory storage; it is constructed out of a series of natural wood ladders and pine shelves. The nest of drawers, originally intended for filing, is just deep enough to take a folded shirt. The 'Dinco' kitchen chair by Lusty was one of the most economical chairs available in 1957.

Below
A 1957 shoot shows (*clockwise from top left*): a 'U60' settee from Lebus; a stick-back dining chair from Cintique; 'Antelope' side table by Ernest Race and open-armed armchair by Cintique; occasional table by Vanson; 'Ketley' armchair by Parker Knoll; '369A' stick-back chair by Ercol.

subsequently became known for his designs for Knoll.

As well as American-based designers, there was a strong Scandinavian influence on furniture during the Fifties; the two best-known designers were Arne Jacobsen and Eero Saarinen. Arne Jacobsen was a Danish architect and designer; his most instantly recognizable piece of furniture is his cleverly curved 'Egg' chair. Other Jacobsen designs that are still popular today include the 'Series 7' chair, 'Swan' chair and 'Ant' chair. Despite using cutting-edge technology to create his chairs – which were often in metal and plastic – he drew on organic shapes and forms for inspiration. The same went for Eero Saarinen, a Finnish designer and architect who emigrated to the States when he was 13. His 'Tulip' chair and 'Saarinen' table both appeared in 1956 and were iconic pieces of Fifties furniture, with fluid shapes that were both simple and stylish.

Other important contributors to the development of furniture during this decade include the Italian designer Giò Ponti, whose 'Superleggera' chair, made of varnished ash with a cane seat, was a pared-back, elegant version of a traditional design – an example of how modern furniture could reinvent what had gone before. French designer Jean Prouvé created industrial-inspired, simple pieces that were masterpieces of functional, economical design. While home-grown companies were still the most popular with the general public, the wealth of international talent gradually seeped through into every element of furniture, and created what we now think of as the Fifties interior.

'ARMCHAIR TIMES'

NOVEMBER 1958

Below left
The 'S6724' easy chair, designed by Martin Grierson, took the shape of an aeroplane seat as inspiration and was manufactured by Heal's.

Below right
'B415' G Plan wing chair by Gomme.

'I do think Anne is taking that old gag about "two can live as cheaply as one" a bit far. What else can one do in this blissful chair? Away with ambition! Step off the treadmill! Cry Halt to the rat race!'

'Thank heavens these armchair chaps are beginning to design chairs with strong high backs for tall chaps like me'

Top row
From left to right, 'S6724' as before;
'Piquante' designed by Ward and Austen,
from Buoyant; and 'Eden', by Cintique.

Middle row
From left to right, 'Rome' by Christie-Tyler,
from William Perring; 'UC6' by Conran
Furniture; and 'Bianca' by Wood Bros,
from Heal's.

Bottom row
From left to right, 'Coconut' by George
Nelson, from Hille; 'Angelina' by Wood Bros,
from Heal's; and 'Isis' by Robert Heritage,
from George Stone.

Below
'Delfino' chair by Erberto Carboni,
complete with matching footstool.

Right
'R57' armchair by Ernest Race.

*'Oh what a joy to relax in a brand new chair with
such a convenient footrest'*

*'Such a delicious chair. Good firm back. Length just right for my legs.
Well-shaped arms, and Richard always longing to take over'*

'SOFAS:
GUIDE TO GRACEFUL
LAYABOUTING'

JULY 1959

'An armchair is all very well, but oh, the
extra-sensory bliss of a really well-
designed, well-sprung, well-enclosed
sofa, with its invitations to gossip
(or rather, conversational exchanges),
but at its best when the solitary
traveller wearily returns to the nest and
finds the sofa, the whole sofa, his
(or hers) alone'

Left
From top, 'Flamingo' two-seater sofa with mahogany legs by Ernest Race, from Heal's; and 'Omega' two-seater sofa by HK.

Below
From top, back view of the 'Flamingo' sofa by Ernest Race, from Heal's; and 'Orpheus 90' four-seater sofa by R S Stevens.

'The range these days is fabulous. You can, you see, return to Oxonian wicker, take refuge in a curving Scandinavian canopy, or a deep Italian cloudland defying its spiky legs, sit up more formally in a modern bergère, recline adamantinely in a specimen originally designed for a three-part conversazione'

'DESK:
EVERY HOUSE NEEDS A DESK BUT DOES THE DOMESTIC DESK NEED ANOTHER WORD?'

JANUARY 1959

'How useful for David to have a desk and me to have a storage cabinet and a bookcase and a bureau – and a really outstanding, upstanding flower stand. I do hope David won't mind'

'Oh how sensible I was to get a desk with such deliciously streamlined legs – if you see what I mean, of course'

Far left
'K9143' Danish teak-veneered bookcase and desk from Heal's.

Left
'30/5001' teak-veneered writing table with ebonized finish from Liberty.

Below
'Junior Secretary (D4/A)' desk and 'C10' chair by Conran Furniture.

'I used to be the angriest angry man in Budleigh Salterton – until I got this brand-new spanking desk. Now I'm already well into the fifteenth chapter of my new novel about the revolt of the earthworms. So much more relaxing and rewarding!'

Below left
Antique French *bonheur du jour* in mahogany from General Trading Co. The chair is upholstered in red damask and is from Liberty.

Below right
This 'Desk 2600' by LM Furniture is mahogany with a beech frame. The Danish chair is by Finmar.

Following pages
House & Garden's colour range from 1958 (*left*). A 1955 couple choose a wallpaper to complement a modern painting (*right*). The lights are from Hiscock Appleby, and the cotton rug is from Tumbeltwist. The black stick-back dining chair is from Finmar, and to the left of it is a 'Telechair' from Hille, with cups and saucers from Holiday Studioware.

'I always knew that once I got a really beautiful desk even my answers in the negative would have the most exquisitely endearing touch, don't you think?'

'Dear Mummy, I don't somehow think the 26th is going to be convenient. Peter isn't looking so well – he's been working so hard at home in the evenings, poor dear – and he thinks he'll be in bed on the 26th with a streamer. So why not put off your visit until sometime next year?'

SWATCH: PATTERNS, COLOURS & TEXTILES

Printed textiles and patterned wallpapers added a vibrancy to the Fifties house. In the years after the Second World War, the 'Britain Can Make It' exhibition in 1946 and the Festival of Britain in 1951 showcased an exciting array of contemporary designs by new designers. These patterns became synonymous with the bold, forward-looking ethos of the Fifties.

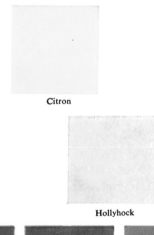

Citron

Hollyhock

Aubergine	Guardsman	Flame	Seville	Siamese Pink	Cardinal	Terracotta	Persimmon
Willow	Bitter Green	Green Olive	Forest	Leaf	Sky Blue		
Gunmetal	Dove Grey	Cloud Grey	Bamboo	Mocha	Sandalwood	Thames Green	Mustard
Hot Chocolate	Deep Night	Dresden Blue	Deep Purple	Cornflower	Cerulean Blue	Kingfisher	

Left
This 1955 couple examine a Crown wallpaper. To the right is a striped Sanderson wallpaper , while amid the mass of fabric on the floor is a rust, brown and white 'Parnassus' by Grafton; 'Crescents' by Heal's in an abstract pattern of grey, white and lime; and a bright-yellow, white and black rayon with a motif in a hand-drawn style from Whitehead.

Below
Melamine canisters and egg cups in 'Forest Green', 'Cardinal', 'Gunmetal', 'Black', 'Cloud Grey' and 'Sage Green'. Enamelled bowls in 'Aubergine', 'Yellow', 'Forest Green', 'Cerulean' and 'Pink', alongside an assortment of candles in the *House & Garden* colour range for 1957.

Bottom
Kitchen chairs in black, yellow and red sit on a tufted carpet in cornflower blue from Rivington. A mirror with an enamelled-pink frame, from Rowley Productions, reflects a '424' chair from Ginsom & Slater. The orange velvet is from Morton Sundour and the 'C9' stool is from Conran.

The Fifties was an exciting time for pattern. Contemporary fabrics and wallpapers sprung up simultaneously in Britain and in the States in an international movement. Abstract designs became very popular and lively colours added vibrancy to designs that often incorporated spiky, freehand lines and shapes. Because the war had caused such a break in production, its aftermath saw a completely new era in pattern design. In Britain, Heal's led the way, buying patterns from freelance designers. Throughout much of the Fifties, these fabrics were roller-printed or hand-screen-printed – the process wasn't properly mechanized until 1959. Lucienne Day was the best-known textile designer of this era, and it was Heal's who put her most famous pattern ,'Calyx', into production, following its debut in an interior set in the Festival of Britain's Homes and Gardens Pavilion, designed by her husband Robin Day. 'Calyx' was an abstract, organic print, with a bright palette that combined strong and earthy hues. Lucienne Day became a regular designer for Heal's, creating patterns that were both imaginative and innovative. She drew on modern artists for inspiration, including the paintings of Joan Miró and Paul Klee, Alexander Calder's mobiles and the cartoons of Saul Steinberg. Over the course of the decade, Day's designs became bolder and more architectural, while still retaining their playful edge.

Below
In this 1958 shoot, Jimmy Edwards, who played the headmaster from popular television series *Whack-O!*, instructed readers on the latest linens. Enveloped in a 'Whitney Point' blanket from Charles Early, the headmaster is surrounded by bedlinen and towels from Haworth, Everwear, Vantona, Lamont and Horrockses.

Right
Colours from the *House & Garden* range from 1953 are used in this dining room. Aside from a splash of 'Citron', courtesy of the lamp shade, the colours are from the palette shown (*below right*), which are, from top: 'Blueberry', 'Cloud Grey', 'Sky Blue' and 'Flame'.

Below
Mustard yellow is the prevailing colour in this 1957 room. The 'Ferdinand' wallpaper is from John Line, while the 'Crusader' Wilton carpet is from S J Stockwell. The yellow silk curtain from Liberty provides a dramatic backdrop for the bamboo Rowland Spillane chair, the tables are from Conran and the kingfisher-blue cockerels are from Fortnum & Mason. The painting is by John Piper.

Below right
A 1957 shopping shoot shows a 'Revo' electric iron and a battery radio from Ekco – both of these were available in a number of different colours. The table lamp and the selection of multicoloured shades are all from Troughton & Young.

Bottom
From the same shoot is a set of table mats in 'Leaf', 'Bitter Green' and 'Dresden Blue', with matching coasters, all from Tibor. The mixing bowls are in 'Lemon Peel', 'Dresden Blue' and 'Willow' – part of the *House & Garden* colour range – and were manufactured by Pyrex.

Below
House & Garden's colour range for 1956 was a noticeable departure from its earlier colour charts of that decade in that it incorporated a lot more softer tones alongside the bolder shades. At this time, more than a hundred manufacturers were producing goods using the *House & Garden* colour range.

Right
The 1955 *House & Garden* colour range introduced five new shades to the existing palette. These are shown on the five eggs at the top of the picture and are, *from left*, 'Cantaloupe', 'Cardinal', 'Clover Pink', 'Mocha' and 'Emerald'.

Day's designs may have formed the backbone of Heal's fabric collections, but the company commissioned a number of other talented designers, such as Michael O'Connell, who created linear patterns in restrained tones, and Mary White, whose prints combined modern abstract shapes with an Arts and Crafts aesthetic.

While Heal's led the way in the Fifties textiles revolution, David Whitehead, of Rawtenstall, Lancashire, was following closely in its footsteps. David Whitehead adopted a similar approach to Heal's in commissioning exciting contemporary designers, but the fabrics cost less. This was the idea of the then-director, John Murray, who wanted to make daring modern designs available to the mass market. David Whitehead's contemporary prints launched in 1951, with vibrant, small-scale patterns roller-printed on cheap spun rayon. The designers included Marian Mahler and Jacqueline Groag, as well as two upcoming young British designers, Roger Nicholson and Terence Conran. An early design of Conran's 'Chequers' was shown at the Festival of Britain and he sold a number of

Left
Small chalk-white flowers and leaf motifs are shown on two Sanderson wallpapers from 1953 in lime green 51511 (*far left*) and flame 51509 (*top centre*). Between them, geometric patterns abound on a sky-blue paper from Crown, the black-and-white hand-drawn 'Check' on a dark-pink ground by Barbara Hirsch at Cole & Son (*centre*) and a gold-and-black

diamond motif from Sanderson (*centre left*). The model holds a flower and leaf design from Crown, also shown in pink and mustard colourways. Just behind her is a Sanderson paper of raised white stars on a midnight-blue ground and a bamboo-fence patterned paper from Crown.

Below
This 1952 shot shows off the many different colours of linoleum available; primary colours were particularly popular. In the UK, Marley, British Mouldex and Williamson's stocked wide ranges of linoleum. The smooth surface of the lino is deliberately emphasized by the rough texture of the sheepskin rug from Morland's.

patterns to David Whitehead during the Fifties, as well as founding his own textiles company, Conran Fabrics, with his wife Shirley. Marian Mahler, who emigrated to Britain from Austria in 1937, was one of David Whitehead's leading designers during the Fifties and created a series of vivid, brightly coloured patterns, some abstract, others incorporating figures, animals and inanimate objects. She had trained at the Kunstgewerbeschule in Vienna, as had another of David Whitehead's designers, the Czech-born Jacqueline Groag.

Liberty commissioned cutting-edge furnishing fabrics for their 'Young Liberty' range. Although its main designers during this decade were Robert Stewart and Colleen Farr, designers including Lucienne Day, Terence Conran and Jacqueline Groag also produced patterns for the company.

In the States, there was a trend for matching wallpaper and fabrics, and although Britain favoured a more eclectic assortment of prints, the link between fabric and wallpaper design was still very strong, with many prints being reproduced across the different mediums. Cole & Son produced contemporary ranges of wallpapers throughout the Fifties, and although they had two prolific in-house designers –

Below
This 1955 display of carpets shows off advances in fibres, colours and textures. Previously, wool was the standard material for carpets, but this selection includes viscose and other synthetic blends, lauded for their durability and their moth-repelling qualities.

Right
Shot among chemistry equipment, this 1957 display shows the versatility of synthetic fabrics, focusing on the range of different textures that rayon and viscose mixes could achieve, ranging from a smooth satin-like finish to a rough hand-woven effect. David Whitehead's screen-printed bark-weave rayon is shown in a monochrome silhouette

design (*centre*) and in grey cross-stripes lifted by a bold orange slash (*right*). The company's harlequin rayon satin (*above centre*) is also featured above the Moygashel 'Finisterre' viscose furnishing fabric in an irregular yellow, pink and green print overlaid with black organic shapes. Two Edinburgh Weavers rayon/cottons (a purple 'Cadenza' and a small turquoise 'Contessa' swatch, *both right*)

further illustrate the versatility of the cellulose fibres used.

William Odell and Henry Skeen – they also bought numerous patterns from freelancers, including Daphne Barder, Barbara Hirsch and June Lyon.

Wall Paper Manufacturers Ltd (WPM) also championed contemporary design, printing patterns by Robert and Roger Nicholson and Lucienne Day. These modern machine-printed designs were marketed under the trade name Crown, and many of these can be seen in the sitting-room and kitchen schemes shown in Part Two of this book. While wallpaper was popular in both plain and patterned varieties, the developments in manufacturing paint had enabled homeowners to gain access to a greater range of shades than ever before. New emulsion paints replaced distemper, which meant that colour could be applied faster, stayed on the wall better and needed only one coat. DIY was popular during the Fifties, and most homeowners would paint their house themselves.

It was largely thanks to *House & Garden* that the trend for using brightly coloured paint on walls and furniture became popular. Throughout the Fifties, *House & Garden* created its own range of paint colours, which it updated annually and marketed through a number of stockists.

Left
With this many carpets, it's no wonder that the maid in this 1957 image looks distressed as she clutches her carpet beater. The display celebrates traditional British Axminster and Wilton carpets. Axminsters include: (1) 'Crown' from J Tempeton, (2) Floral '112/636' from William C Gray, (3) 'Floraform' from Quayle & Tranter, (4) 'Tudor Brocade'

from A F Stoddard, (5) 'Anglia' from Carpet Trades, (6) 'Buckingham' from T F Firth, (7) 'Badgeworth' from The Gloucester Carpet Co. Wilton carpets include (8) 'Regent' from T Bond Worth and all the plain coloured carpets.

Below
A colour scheme built around a reproduction oil painting is enlivened by accents of red in the Woollands rug and the chair imported from Danesco. A pair of E Gomme chests complement the modern, industrial-inspired shelves above, in this 1957 scheme. To the left is a 'Chiavari' chair from Conran. The printed cotton curtain fabric is also from Danesco.

These bright colour wheels reveal a confident attitude to colour that became bolder as the decade went on – the sheer variety of shades on offer were far removed from the restrained muted or neutral shades that had typified the Forties interior.

Despite the radical advances in design and the new, stripped-back modern aesthetic seeping into the home, many people were still resistant to the idea of change and stuck to the dull colour palettes of old. Even as the end of the decade approached, this attitude

lingered on. Luckily *House & Garden* had something to say about it:

'A formidably impressive number of British housewives (abetted by their husbands) still confuse household clutter with a comfortable home. And clutter's staunchest ally is that inimitably British colour combination of seaweed and mud. The rich primaries and their many gay derivatives are suspect. "Too much like that Picasso fellow. After all, fawn and

green are Nature's colours, and they go with anything, don't they?" Well, they don't. Not always, anyway, and Nature also thought up the poppy, the cornflower, and the laburnum.'
—MARCH 1958

The magazine won its battle for bold colour in the end. As the Fifties drew to a close, the foundations had been laid for a new wave of brighter, modern interiors. More was to come. Roll on the Sixties.

PHLOX PINK

SIAMESE PINK

CHERRY

SANDALWOOD

PEBBLE

CLOUD GREY

SAND

DRIFTWOOD

CITRON

SKY BLUE

CERULEAN BLUE

LEMON PEEL

MUSTARD

House & Garden *colours for interior decoration*

FLAME

DOVE GREY

HOT CHOCOLATE

DRESDEN BLUE

NASTURTIUM

GUNMETAL

TERRA COTTA

MIDDY BLUE

CARNATION

BLUEBERRY

WILLOW

GREEN OLIVE

LEAF

FOREST

PORCELAIN BLUE

BITTER GREEN

SPRUCE

Below
This 1953 sitting room was designed using colours from the *House & Garden* range, including contrasting wallpaper with grounds in 'Blueberry' and 'Flame' flanking a pair of curtains in 'Leaf'. The carpet is in 'Gunmetal', while accents of colour are provided by an ottoman upholstered in 'Terracotta' and a 'Siamese Pink' cushion.

BIBLIOGRAPHY & STOCKISTS

Casey, Andrew (2014) *Lucienne Day*, ACC

Harling, Robert (1964) *House & Garden: The Modern Interior*, Condé Nast

House & Garden (1953) *House & Garden's Complete Guide to Interior Decoration* (fifth edition), Simon & Schuster

Hoskins, Lesley (1994) *Fiftiestyle: Home Decoration and Furnishings from the 1950s*, Middlesex University Press

Jackson, Lesley (1994) *Contemporary: Architecture and Interiors and the 1950s*, Phaidon

Jackson, Lesley (2011) *Robin & Lucienne Day: Pioneers of Contemporary Design*, Mitchell Beazley

Jackson, Lesley (1991) *The New Look: Design in the Fifties*, Thames & Hudson

Leighton, Sophie (2009) *The 1950s Home*, Shire Publishing

Lutyens, Dominic (2013) *Living with Mid-century Collectibles*, Ryland Peters & Small

Miller, Judith (2012) *Mid-century Modern: Living with Mid-century Modern Design*, Miller's

Quinn, Bradley (2004) *Mid-century Modern: Interiors, Furniture, Design, Details*, Conran Octopus

Utility Advisory Committe (1947) *Utility Furniture: Catalogue*, Advisory Committee on Utility Furniture

Many of the companies featured in this book are still going strong, while many of the furniture designs remain in production by companies licenced to manufacture them to the original specifications. Where possible, their websites are listed below.

Alessi www.alessi.com

Anglepoise www.anglepoise.com

Buoyant Upholstery www.buoyant-upholstery.co.uk

Cole & Son www.cole-and-son.com

The Conran Shop www.conranshop.co.uk

Crown www.crownpaint.co.uk

Edinburgh Weavers www.edinburghweavers.com

Ercol www.ercol.co.uk

Fornasetti www.fornasetti.com

G Plan www.gplan.co.uk

The General Trading Company www.generaltradingcompany.co.uk

G P & J Baker www.gpandbaker.com

Harrods www.harrods.com

Heal's www.heals.co.uk

Hille www.hille.co.uk

John Lewis www.johnlewis.com

Knoll www.knoll.com

Liberty www.liberty.co.uk

Sanderson www.sanderson-uk.com

Spode www.spode.co.uk

Vitra www.vitra.com

PICTURE CREDITS

Page 1: March 1953
Pages 2 and 3: April 1957
Page 4: June 1952

All photographs by The Condé Nast
Publications Ltd studio photographers
Caradog Williams, Michael Wickham,
Anthony Denney, Hans Hammarskiöld,
John Sadovy and Cyril Readjones except
the following:

Page 4, 16: Scott Hyde

Page 7: Popperfoto/Getty Images

Pages 61, 78, 86, 89: Copyright Norman
   Parkinson Ltd/Courtesy Norman
   Parkinson Archive

Pages 134–7: Fondation Le Corbusier
   © FLC/ ADAGP, Paris and DACS, London
   2014. Photographs by Lucien Hervé. The
   Getty Research Institute, Los Angeles,
   © J. Paul Getty Trust

Pages 142–5: Rhys-Dorvyne

Pages 150–3: Guy Gravett

Pages 154–7: © 2014 Eames Office, LLC
   (eamesoffice.com). Photographs courtesy
   of the Library of Congress, Prints and
   Photographs Division

Page 158: Paul Popper/Popperfoto/
   Getty Images

Pages 168–71: courtesy of Università Iuav
   di Venezia – Archivio Progetti, Fondo
   Giorgio Casali

Pages 172–7: © Ezra Stoller/Esto

INDEX

INDEX

An Hachette UK Company
www.hachette.co.uk

First published in Great Britain in 2014
by Conran Octopus,
a division of Octopus Publishing Group Ltd
Endeavour House
189 Shaftesbury Avenue
London
WC2H 8JY
www.octopusbooks.co.uk
www.octopusbooksusa.com

Distributed in the US by
Hachette Book Group
1290 Avenue of the Americas
4th and 5th Floors
New York, NY 10020

Distributed in Canada by
Canadian Manda Group
664 Annette St.
Toronto, Ontario, Canada M6S 2C8

Text copyright © The Condé Nast
Publications Ltd 2014
Design and layout copyright © Octopus
Publishing Group Ltd 2014

House & Garden registered trademark is
owned by The Condé Nast Publications
Limited and is used under licence from it.
All rights reserved.

All rights reserved. No part of this work may
be reproduced or utilized in any form or by
any means, electronic or mechanical,
including photocopying, recording or by any
information storage and retrieval system,
without the prior written permission of the
publisher.

The right of Catriona Gray to be identified as
the author of this Work has been asserted in
accordance with the Copyright, Designs and
Patents Act 1988.

ISBN 978 1 84091 662 1

A CIP catalogue record for this book is
available from the British Library

Printed and bound in China

10 9 8 7 6 5 4 3 2 1

Every effort has been made to reproduce
the colours in this book accurately; however,
the printing process can lead to some
discrepancies. The colour samples provided
should be used as a guideline only.

Publisher Alison Starling
Editor Pauline Bache
Art Director Jonathan Christie
Production Manager Katherine Hockley

Special thanks to:
Harriet Wilson, Brett Croft and Ben Evans
at The Condé Nast Publications Ltd.

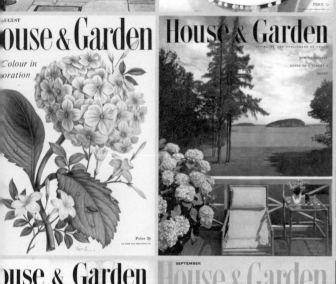

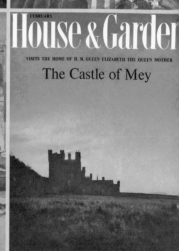